"Gary Meadors's new book, *Decisi*
and thoughtful approach to one of
sonally found the book to be truly
(his weak brother, strong brother
and his overall thesis to be quite compelling. As we enter the post
modern age with its confusion as to how to incorporate the Bible
into picture, Dr. Meadors's challenge that it remains foundational
for the quest is a helpful reminder and challenge."

—Martin G. Abegg Jr., Ph.D., professor, Trinity Western University

"In Decision Making God's Way, Gary Meadors frees us from seeing
God's will as a burden or mystery, to the joyful embrace of God's
will as a pattern of life. God's will is a transformed mind rooted in a
Christian worldview and biblical values. With theological precision
and practical insight, Meadors helps us to discern that the divine will
is ultimately about God's moral will, from which we then approach
every day decisions that face us. A welcomed and readable contribution to the literature on God's will."

—Dennis P. Hollinger, Ph.D., vice provost and professor,
Messiah College

"In this thought-provoking work, Gary Meadors presents well the
view that finding God's will involves applying godly discernment
rather than figuring out in advance the sovereign plan of God. The
message that comes through loud and clear is that it is impossible
to know the will of God without first knowing God, without studying his Word, viewing the world from his perspective, and taking
on his values."

—Dr. Joel F. Williams, professor, Columbia International University

"Finally, a book that deals with decision making that is informed
by both biblical Theology and Christian Worldview considerations.
It is without peer in this literature in being biblically solid, philo-
sophically informed and practically useful. Written for the discern
ing reader, it is a distinctive and welcome addition to this recurrent
discussion."

—Dr. James M. Grier, professor, Grand Rapids Baptist Seminary

Decision Making
God's Way

A New Model for Knowing God's Will

Gary T. Meadors

Baker Books

A Division of Baker Book House Co
Grand Rapids, Michigan 49516

© 2003 by Gary T. Meadors

Published by Baker Books
a division of Baker Book House Company
P.O. Box 6287, Grand Rapids, MI 49516-6287
www.bakerbooks.com

Printed in the United States of America

Library of Congress Cataloging-in-Publication Data
Meadors, Gary T., 1945–
    Decision making God's way : a new model for knowing God's will / Gary T. Meadors.
        p.   cm.
    Includes bibliographical references.
    ISBN 0-8010-6429-5 (pbk.)
    1. Christian life. 2. God—Will. I. Title.
BV4501.3.M43 2003
248.4—dc21   2003010491

For
Gloria
and
Rex and Lori

Contents

Part 4 Reflections on God's Will Applied

Preface

The ideas presented in this book have taken shape over a long period of time. My study of the Bible and my observations about life have slowly merged into a model for discerning God's will in the daily decisions confronting us. I have shared these ideas in church and classroom settings, and the encouraging responses motivated the birth of this book.

Someone once stated, "Creativity is not so much a matter of content as it is of individual treatment." This book treats the biblical passages and ideas that most books on God's will include; however, the model I present is unique. I hope that a new way of looking at discerning God's will for the decisions you face will make you a better decision maker.

As an author, I am indebted to all I have read and to the persons with whom I have conversed about this subject. To mention only a few of those who have helped me along the way runs the risk of omitting some who should be referenced. I do need, however, to make special note of a few who helped shape my thinking by reviewing various drafts of this volume. My colleagues Mark Lamport, John Ver-Berkmoes, Rex Rogers, James Grier, George Zemek, and Mike Rohwer provided many helpful insights. Thanks also to Keith DeBoer and Tim Detweiler for comments from a test run in the Sunday school of my local church. My students Micah Roberts and Scott Thomas provided special help in charting some ideas into PowerPoint slides. Special appreciation is due my wife, Gloria, for reading a variety of drafts and sacrificing family time during the writing of this book. I also benefited greatly from the fine editorial guidance of my editor at Baker Books, Vicki Crumpton.

This book would never have been possible without the generous grant that I received from the Believer's Foundation. Thank you, Steven and Ken, for initiating the grant process and helping me bring this project to fruition.

Introduction

In 1966 I had just been discharged from the navy and was on my way to college in Roanoke, Virginia. During my time in the service, I became a Christian and decided that my calling in life was to prepare for a vocational Christian career. Finally I would begin the journey toward school and full-time ministry. During my first semester, a young lady named Gloria captured my attention. We had met briefly at a Christian Servicemen's Center in Norfolk and discovered that we were going to the same school. Once at college, I observed Gloria's ease with people. She stood out to me because I was a loner and felt awkward in social relationships. I saw how she could add a dimension to my future ministry, and I asked her for a date. We became engaged on our second date, although she put me off a couple of days before saying yes! She wrote home with the news and informed me that her parents would visit us the next weekend.

Gloria's father had been a Christian only about ten years. Prior to his conversion, he lived a very rough life, and he still had a rough-cut exterior. When they arrived, he put

Gloria and his wife in the backseat of the car and me in the front. For two days he grilled me about this whirlwind engagement and why I thought I should marry his daughter. At the midnight hour, when all seemed lost, I blurted out, "We are getting married because it is God's will." That effectively ended the discussion. Gloria's father was now a happy camper, and I was relieved that the inquisition was over. After that comment, Dad never asked another question, because the divine seal of approval for making a decision had been pronounced—"It is God's will." Who can argue with such a statement?

A lot of water has gone under the bridge since that day. My wife and I recently celebrated our thirty-fifth wedding anniversary. The decision we made has proved to be a good one. But if I were in my father-in-law's driver's seat today, I certainly would reflect on the question of God's will in a more objective way than I did at that time. How would you critique this whirlwind relationship? What questions would you ask if you were Gloria's father? What answers would you accept? What *values* were driving my decision-making process at that time, whether I was aware of them or not? I think I had some selfish values as well as good ones. What were they? Is the self-claim that "it is God's will" adequate to justify a decision? How do you even know if something is God's will?

I am sure you have asked yourself, "What is God's will for my life?" Perhaps you were reflecting on career choices, who to marry, where to live, or how far to extend yourself to purchase a home. Maybe you had a job change opportunity that provided career advancement but brought conflict into your family because of the potential interruption in your lifestyle. Have you ever found yourself struggling to explain why God "changed his mind" about a course of action you previously followed dogmatically, yet now you find yourself looking in a new direction? How do you process the decisions life brings to you on a daily basis? All Christians struggle with knowing God's will. We often seek a sense of certainty in our efforts to discern life's decisions even as we pray and endeavor to live a godly life.

The goal of *Decision Making God's Way* is to help you learn to discern life's decisions and gain confidence in the process. Knowing God's will about the issues of life confronting you is primarily a process of clarifying life's questions and challenges from a biblical worldview and values set. The following chapters will show you how your worldview and values affect Christian discernment. You will enlarge your capacity to think critically about God's will for your life within the biblical framework that God has already given you. You will be encouraged to create and evaluate your values from a biblical perspective and apply them to the issues and decisions confronting you. Such a perspective teaches you to deal with life rather than be a victim of subjective processes and the voices demanding that you conform to "their" view of things.

The Big Picture

Developing a model for discerning God's will is like trying to build a skyscraper in one day. You cannot do it! A sequence of steps is required to construct a good building or to produce a model of discernment. The analogy breaks down a bit at this point, however. A physical building must proceed from bottom to top. A mental framework is a bit more complicated. For example, this book could begin with a treatment of specific Bible verses about God's will. This would be an analytical approach, akin to studying individual trees before we know the forest in which we are located. Or, we could begin with the big picture so that we can see the whole forest—a synthetic method identifies the forest so we can recognize the trees as we encounter them. A synthesis starts with the big idea and then becomes more specific, in this case studying the biblical passages to understand the genesis of the big idea.

Decision Making God's Way moves from synthesis to analysis. For example, a classic text on the will of God is Romans 12:1–2: "Be transformed by the renewing of your mind. Then you will be able to test and approve what God's will is." This statement raises some foundational issues for our quest to know God's will. The fact that we need a transformed mind indicates that we already have a problem! It also implies that we have a responsibility to think and act. Our "problem of knowing" will be identified along with the solution God has provided. Because the mind needs to be transformed, we must know how we process life's decisions. How do we think about things? How did our worldview and values develop?

I want to help you grow as a reflective Christian so that you can gain confidence in your walk with God. I hope that you will begin to process your decisions within an objective framework of values rather than merely "feeling" your way along.

Chapter Previews

Chapters 1–3 establish foundations for thinking about God's will. We begin by recognizing that God created us in his image. Adam was not a robot, but was created to make decisions guided by God's direct teaching. Adam failed in his task and thereby passed to his descendents the same propensity. Although our task is complicated by the results of sin, our basic responsibility is the same. We are to live life on the basis of God's revealed truth. We will also look closely at why we have a problem knowing God and his will, how God has addressed the problem, and what we can do to establish patterns for reflecting on God's will in light of biblical values.

Chapters 4–6 survey what the Bible actually says about knowing and doing God's will. We will search the Old and New Testaments to discover how each generation of believers has dealt with the quest to know God and his will. And we will delineate the difference between moral obligation and our opportunity to *choose* a course of action within established boundaries.

Chapter 7 emphasizes our responsibility to practice godly discernment in everyday decisions, surfacing God's will for us. Discerning God's will requires reading the Bible as a whole book and not just as a source for a "proof text" to justify a decision.

After the more objective issues of knowing God's will have been established, chapters 8–10 evaluate some of the "inner voices" of guidance. The role of "feelings," conscience, and the Holy Spirit are difficult to discern. These voices become clearer after the foundations and biblical patterns of guidance are identified. The book concludes with questions and answers that illustrate the model presented.

The fact that you have chosen to read this book indicates that you are a serious and thoughtful Christian. I hope your journey through this volume will make you a more reflective Christian who takes ownership in processing life's decisions.

Part 1

Foundations for Knowing God's Will

Christian confessions affirm the Bible as sufficient for faith and practice. With this affirmation comes the assumption that the Bible addresses any question or need we may ever have. Then eventually we leave home, have a problem, run to the Bible, and feel as if we cannot find the answers we were promised. This crisis drives some young adults to relegate the Bible to "religious activity" and look elsewhere for guidance in their daily decisions. More commonly, however, it drives sincere Christians to become subjective in understanding God's guidance in their lives. Such is the case when we claim to know God's will about a matter but we cannot give clear biblical reasoning for how we know what we claim to know.

Chapter 1 probes the Bible's explanation of our problem in knowing God and his will. While we were created in God's image to glorify God by being good decision makers, Adam's sin and its consequences ruined our opportunity. God in his grace, however, addressed our problem by revealing himself and his will to various generations of believers. The supreme product of God's revealing acts is the Bible.

Chapter 2 points out that God expects us to change the way we think so that we can deal with our world. Romans 12:1–2 calls us to transform our minds so that our thinking reflects God's teaching. We need not only to know the command expectations of the Bible but also to develop a biblical worldview and values set so that we can answer the questions that a single Bible verse does not address. Throughout this book I use the phrase "transformed mind," capturing the end product of Paul's exhortation "to be transformed by the renewing of your mind." The mind is the gateway for all change, both cognitive and moral. Once we have gained knowledge, however, we must exercise our "will" to bring our practice into conformity with what we know.

Chapter 3 illustrates how a biblical worldview and values model processes life's decisions. Then, with an overview of our problem and God's solution, we will discover how the Bible's specific statements about God's will work better within a biblical values model than in the typical subjective models.

Knowing God   1

■ "Houston, we have a problem." This is the classic statement from Captain James Lovell, commander of Apollo
13, during a live television broadcast on April 14, 1970.
Captain Lovell's words set in motion an intense rescue
scenario that guided the crew safely back to earth, landing
them in the Pacific Ocean on April 17. It was a harrowing
three-day experience that captured the world's attention
on television.

If Houston can rescue a space capsule and deliver its
crew from what appeared to be certain death, why is it
that when Christians cry out, "God, we have a problem,"
the other end of the phone sometimes seems silent? Most
of us believe that God knows everything and that he loves
us. Therefore, it seems reasonable that God should provide
immediate direction to his children when we call for help.
Why, then, do we often struggle with knowing God's will
for our lives? Life seems like a maze that challenges us to

move from the entrance to the exit without getting caught in dead-end paths. Inside the maze, we only see walls and turns. God stands above the maze and looks down on our plight. He knows the right path. Yet we often find him silent as we evaluate the crossroads we confront. Or, we thought we heard him say, "Turn left," only to find ourselves in a box canyon and in the dilemma of explaining the wrong direction we credited to God. How do we balance the reality of life we experience with good theology?

Seeking God's will for a particular decision begins a journey into one of the most basic yet profound issues in the development of a Christian worldview. What can we know? How do we know what we can know? How does God communicate knowledge to us? These kinds of questions relate to what philosophers and theologians refer to as "epistemology." Epistemology is the study of the sources, nature, and validity of knowledge. It is essential to think about these questions as a foundation for discussing how we know God's will for our lives. This chapter will help you to see the big picture of this problem, how God has addressed the problem, and how God's people in the record of Scripture have pursued life in spite of the challenge to know God and his ways.

How Do We Know Things?

How do we gain knowledge of our world? Let's begin with the world in general. Philosophers recognize four ways that we know what we know. These include sense perception, reason, authority, and intuition.

Our senses of sight, hearing, smell, taste, and touch help us know our world. How many times have you said, "When I see it I will believe it!" This statement means that when I actually see an event for myself, I will then know that it is true and worthy of belief. (On the other hand, a blind person knows the world by touch, smell, and hearing, senses that are often intensified when sight is not present.) If someone says it is cold outside, we might go out the door to feel just how cold it is. We confirm some claims about reality with our senses in order to gain knowledge. Sense perception is more objective by nature. That is, senses are not merely internal feelings or hunches without something concrete to back them up. To confirm knowledge by the senses requires an objectively observable setting.

Sense perception alone, however, is not adequate for all knowledge. Consider the following illustration. I once heard a joke about a Quaker and an atheist. Quakers are known to stress their experience of knowing God. A certain atheist wanted to demonstrate a Quaker's inability to prove that God existed so he asked a series of questions.

"Ms. Quaker, have you ever seen God?"

"I see him in his creation," she replied.

"That does not count," countered the atheist. "Creation could be the product of evolution."

"Well then," she replied, "if you mean have I ever seen God in physical form, I would have to say no, I have not seen God."

"Ah ha," said the atheist. "Have you ever touched God?"

"I see," she replied, "that you are insisting that I can only know God by direct sense perception. By that test, I would have to say that I have never touched God."

The atheist was feeling very proud of himself and blurted out in disgust, "Well then, have you ever smelled God!"

"No," she meekly replied.

"Therefore, Ms. Quaker, I have to conclude that you have no God."

Then she replied, "Mr. Atheist, might I ask you some questions?"

"Of course," he arrogantly answered.

"Mr. Atheist, have you ever seen your brain?"

"I see the product of my brain in thinking," he responded sharply.

"Now, Mr. Atheist, you would not allow me the privilege of implicational evidence, so that will not count for you either. Mr. Atheist, have you ever touched your brain?"

"This is ridiculous," he replied. "What is your point?"

"Well, Mr. Atheist, on the basis of your model of how to know something exists, and since you have never seen or touched your brain, I can only conclude that you have no brain!"

This humorous story illustrates that knowledge is more complicated than simple sensory perception. Knowing something requires the ability to reason from point A to point B, to delineate between evidence and implication. We can sense that it is raining outside when a feeling of wet corresponds with our sense of touch. Or we might hear the sound of rain and conclude by the sense of hearing and reason that it is raining. But to know whether a brain or God exists requires a coherent reasoning process beyond the senses.

Sense perception and reason are the two primary sources for obtaining knowledge about our world. Secondary sources include authority and intuition. Most of us know what we know because someone we trust told us, "This is the way it is." Authority as a source of knowledge organizes our world until we mature and make our own decisions. Then we become an authority to someone else! Authority may also originate from a group (e.g., creationists, evolutionists, postmodernists) that has determined through the senses and reason that the world should be interpreted in a certain way. Such groups develop worldviews that provide different sets of presuppositions, giving their followers a framework to explain their world. This illustrates why humanity can have very different answers for the same set of questions. Divergent proposals explaining "what we know" result in conflicting and competing views.

Intuition is "the direct apprehension of knowledge that is not the result of conscious reasoning or of immediate sense perception."[1] Intuition might be claimed for something as simple as my self-awareness of things that I know by the senses or reason. If I hear a police siren, I now know intuitively what I learned by other means. Some refer to intuition to explain how our accumulated knowledge and experience can converge unconsciously and cause a thought or insight to come to us. This accounts for the "unexpected" insights that sometimes come to scientists, teachers, writers, poets, factory workers, and all manner of persons who work for years in a certain setting. Intuition also explains the mystical knowledge claimed by many types of religions. It is a direct apprehension of knowledge that cannot be accounted for by the senses or reason. Because intuition tends to be of a more subjective nature, it is precarious to allow it to be our only source of knowing something. We should test our intuitions by the more objective sources of knowledge.

Clearly, we know things in many different ways. We might use our external senses or the process of reason, or we might lean on intuition or some authority we trust to provide us with knowledge. Usually, no one source is adequate in and of itself. The knowledge these sources provide collectively gives us a foundation in our quest to understand our world. The questions about life that trouble us, however, do not always seem to be clarified by the more objective processes. For example, a young person comes to you and says, "You know that Kelly and I have been dating for some time and that we really like each other. Do you think we are in love? How do I know if she is the one? How do I know that it is love and not just friendship?" Or maybe you have struggled with choosing between various job options or churches to attend. The options all seem to be acceptable, but you want certainty. You want to know if one is more *God's will* for you than another. How do you decide between seemingly equal options? My experience is that most people struggle with finding a confident answer to these kinds of questions. I hope to demonstrate, however, that you should be able to think through the scenarios life presents, and I hope to provide an objective analysis that will lead you to appropriate and God-honoring answers. But first let us review how the Bible presents the problem of knowing.

Know the Bible to Know the World

We need to review the biblical story about the problem of knowing in order to explain the state of our world.

Created in the Image of God

Before we focus on the problem of knowing God's will after Adam's sin in Eden, let's consider God's original design for humankind. Although Genesis 1–3 is brief, we find some significant implications about God's intentions for Adam and the human race. We are introduced to humans on the sixth day when God said, "Let us make man in our image, in our likeness, and let them rule over [the earth]" (Gen. 1:26). Humans are the closest to being like God than any other category of creation. We were designed in the image of God in such a way that we especially reflect and represent the Creator in his creation. We were particularly created for God's glory (Isa. 43:7; Rom. 11:36), and the chief goal of men and women is to glorify God (1 Cor. 10:31).

Theologians discuss a variety of issues about what it means to be created in God's image. We are particularly unique in our capacity for critical self-reflection and moral responsibility. Animals surely have some level of thinking and feeling capability. You know this if you own a pet! But my dogs have never demonstrated the critical thinking skills to let themselves out and get their own food, even when doing so would require little reflection. The ability to think critically and do right are premiere reflections of our Creator. Who we become as persons and how we operate in our world provide either a good or bad reflection of our Father in heaven.

But how did God design the measure of whether we are a good or bad reflection of him? Consider what little we know about Adam in the original Eden. The fuller summary of Genesis 2:15–25 offers a few pointers. God gave Adam some simple directions. He commanded that his creation work the garden and feed himself at his own discretion, and the tree of the knowledge of good and evil was off-limits. These directions constituted God's will for Adam. They created a context in which Adam could make decisions and express himself within God's set parameters. Adam received adequate information so that he could make good judgments. He was responsible to act without being micromanaged. Although Adam was originally without sin, he needed time for moral development. His moral development progressed just like ours. He was to obey God's instructions and reason from them in his daily decisions.

The relationship between God and Adam is much like the created bond of mother and daughter or father and son. Parents provide their children with the parameters that constitute acceptable standards in their family unit. These are often intentionally broad because a parent wants the child to learn to think, "What will please my mother and father?" Children need fences and space to develop. God the Father set the original model by providing Adam with both. Children's following the will of their parents involves two levels. They must (1) exercise raw obedience to the non-negotiable standards and (2) learn how to anticipate the parents' desires by reasoning through what they already know and applying that to the decision they are about to make. This second area thrills the parents. When children, by their own reasoning and will, reflect the expectations of the parents, there is no greater joy on the part of the parents. God designed that Adam and all humankind glorify him in a similar manner. He wants us to respond to his directions, to make choices without being micromanaged, and to make progress in becoming like our Father. The model is one of parent and child, not employer and employee.

Genesis implies more about what God expected from Adam. In the context of Genesis 2:18–25, it seems God used Adam's naming of the animals to cause Adam to come to the realization that life is two by two, not one by one. After using his tremendous intuitive reasoning to characterize the animals by names, perhaps Adam noticed that all created kinds had a Mr. and Mrs. except for his own! God knew this already (2:18), but he set the environment in which Adam came to this conclusion himself. Adam's skills of inductive reasoning were cultivated.

How long did the paradise of Eden last? Nobody knows. I think it was rather brief. It was at least long enough for Adam and Eve to have some conversations about that tree of the knowledge of good and evil. Otherwise, how did Eve add the proviso "you must not touch it" (3:3) to God's statement that "you must not eat from the tree"? It seems that they had taken the context of the tree in the garden to another level.

After two chapters in Genesis, paradise is over. The rest of the Bible describes the aftermath of Adam's sin. We now see that the fall brought distortion to our ability to know God and even ourselves. The ability to glorify God through our obedience to his revealed truth has been aggravated by our participation in humanity's fall from paradise. But alas, all is not lost. Though the fall brought distortion to our being created in his image, clearly we carry on as image bearers (see Gen. 9:6; James 3:9). While it is now harder for us to obey (Rom. 7), it is not impossible. In fact, God demands our obedience. Romans 12:1–2 reminds us of our responsibility to be transformed by the renewing of our minds. This merely means that we are now to think about what it means to conform to God's expectations in an unfriendly world. We therefore do the will of God as we come to understand how biblical truth applies to our everyday lives. In fact, our moral development is a biblical theme of hope, for when we see Jesus, we will be like him (Rom. 8:29; 1 Cor. 15:49; 1 John 3:2). Our likeness to Jesus is a moral likeness that is the product of obedience to God's teaching. This is what doing God's will is all about.

How God dealt with Adam is reflected in his dealing with persons throughout the Bible. Studying the nature of this relationship sets the stage for how God operates with us. We now need to turn to a more comprehensive review of how the consequences of Adam's sin affects our ability to know God and his will.

Paradise Lost . . . Living in the Aftermath

Maybe you have wondered why God put that tree in the garden, especially since he knew the path his human creation would take. It is not a coincidence that this was the tree of the *knowledge* of good and evil (Gen. 2:15–17). The lure of the tree was to know as God knows. The serpent worked this angle well, tempting Adam and Eve to "be like God, knowing good and evil" (Gen. 3:5). At this point in time, Adam and Eve had not yet disobeyed God. In spite of their privileged position, they still fell for the illusion that they could bypass God's design for gaining knowledge. Genesis teaches us that after Adam's rebellion, Adam and his descendents began a new struggle to know God and his will.

What does the Bible have to say about the problem of knowing? Following Adam's failure, the Bible presents a story about the quest to know God and his will for his creation! The record of this story in the Bible is framed in four major movements: creation, fall, redemption, and consummation. Think about how these themes permeate the Bible. Genesis begins the Bible with the story of creation, and Revelation ends with the account of end times and the consummation of history on earth. The burden from Genesis 3 through Revelation is to give creation an opportunity to enter into a redemptive relationship with the Creator, a need resulting from Adam's sin, the fall. An understanding of these four themes within the biblical story is required to interpret God's work in the world.

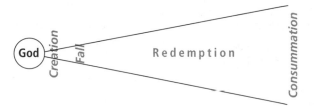

Fig. 1. The Biblical Story

The Old and New Testaments are also self-contained within these themes. Genesis is a book of beginnings. But by the end of the Old Testament, the prophets moan the failure of the world to respond to God's message. They look off into the future to a consummation of earth history when God will set things in order. These same themes are reworked in the New Testament. The Gospels present a new beginning with Christ. John 1 particularly views Christ as the Creator who comes to redeem the world. Yet Christ is crucified by a fallen world that will not respond to God. The apostles pick up the themes and proclaim to their audiences this same understanding of God's will for the world. Yet the world does not hear. Therefore, the Book of Revelation, like the Old Testament prophets, presents divine intervention as the only hope to consummate earth history.

You can see that whether we look at the whole Bible or the Old and New Testaments respectively, the story line is the same. God created the world to know and have fellowship with him. Adam and Eve failed the test that determined our destiny. God in his grace began to pursue his creation in order to bring those who respond back into an originally intended relationship with him. This pursuit has not yet achieved full success, but God continues the pursuit until the day he has appointed to consummate his plan. The Book of Revelation reflects the end result when believing humanity once again enjoys being in God's presence in the New Jerusalem with, interestingly, its river and tree of life (Revelation 21–22).

Interwoven within this story of earth history is the quest of the redeemed to know God. The quest is hampered, however, by the consequences of the fall. The events in Eden short-circuited our ability to know God immediately and accurately. Because discerning God's will requires that we address how we know what we know, we need to understand how Adam's sin has affected our ability to know God. Romans 12:1–2 asserts that we need a "transformed mind" in order to pursue God's will. This need confirms that we have a problem.

In Adam's Fall, We Sinned All

The biblical story of the fall in Genesis is the reason behind a number of the consequences of Adam's sin imposed upon the human race. In the biblical story, physical and spiritual death is attributed to the fall (Rom. 5:12–14). Adam's exclusion from the Garden of Eden presents the image of humanity's exclusion from the presence of God as a normal way of operating. After the fall, men and women are portrayed as inclined to evil. We possess a depraved human nature, and our ability to reason about God has been darkened. Our conscience is not able to make true judgments, or is easily distorted, because the value system to which it responds has been corrupted. The Bible teaches that because all have sinned, all participate in distorted understandings of God. This is our dilemma. This is what we must overcome in order to make good decisions about God's will. We will discuss the solution to this problem, but we must first convince ourselves that we have a problem and that it impacts our quest to know God's will.

The biblical testimony confirms our dilemma. The summary in Genesis 6:5–6 captures the plight of humanity at an early stage: "The LORD saw how great man's wickedness on the earth had become, and that every inclination of the thoughts of his heart was only evil all the time. The LORD was grieved that he had made man on the earth, and his heart was filled with pain" (cf. 8:21). Please note in this text how the term *heart* is a synonym for *mind*. This is true throughout the Bible. Hundreds of years later, King David reflected upon his own sinful behavior and then remarked, "Surely I was sinful at birth, sinful from the time my mother conceived me" (Ps. 51:5). David attributed his own moral problem to the fact that he participated in the results of Adam's sin and therefore chose paths contrary to God's will. This is also true for you and me. We can observe how we are prone from birth to do wrong by observing "innocent" children. Perhaps you have a younger brother or sister. Did you ever tell them, "Don't do that!" Did they do it anyway? Why do we spend most of our time raising children to do right rather than wrong, to make good judgments rather than careless or bad ones? Have you ever seen a book on how to raise bad children? The very patterns of life confirm that at the core of our lives there is a propensity to go our own way. What is true for children is also true for adults. Adults are simply more sophisticated.

At the end of the Old Testament period, the prophets reviewed Israel's behavior and declared it contrary to God's will. The prophets were "covenant police." They examined the revealed will of God in the stipulations of law and the implications of it for daily living and proclaimed Israel an abysmal failure. Isaiah declared, "All of us have become like one who is unclean, and all our righteous acts are like filthy rags" (64:6). Jeremiah chimed in with "The heart is deceitful above all things and beyond cure. Who can understand it?" (17:9; see also 7:24). In Hosea, God connected the problem back to Eden by saying, "Like Adam, they have broken the covenant—they were unfaithful to me there" (6:7).

The New Testament continues the theme of the consequences of the fall in bold relief. Romans 1–3 nails the human coffin closed with a series of Old Testament quotations, culminating in "All have sinned and come short of the glory of God" (3:23). Ephesians declares that all "are darkened in their understanding and separated from the life of God because of the ignorance that is in them due to the hardening of their hearts" (4:18). Paul is addressing the state of the Gentiles and therefore a believer's pre-Christ life. The effects of sin, however, are no less prevalent in the lives of *believers* when they refuse to hear God's teaching. Paul made this clear to the Corinthians in regard to their rejection of revealed truth when he called them immature and carnal in their thinking (1 Cor. 1–3; 14:37–38). Moving from darkened to enlightened thinking requires a conscious, focused transformation of the way we think about our world and ourselves (Rom. 12:1–2).

Scripture highlights the results of this problem as an issue of *what* we know and *how* we know it. That is, the problem of sin affects our ability to know God and his will, and therefore we will have to look outside ourselves for another solution to knowing. Deuteronomy 29:29 declares that "The secret things belong to the LORD our God, but the things revealed belong to us and to our children forever, that we may follow all the words of the law." Knowledge is now conditioned on the basis of whether God chooses to reveal it. In the Old Testament, God's children were given adequate instructions (the law) about living, and they proceeded to order their lives on that basis. Proverbs follows up on this by saying, "Where there is no revelation, the people cast off restraint; but blessed is he who keeps the law" (29:18). Ecclesiastes reflects on the fact that "no man knows the future," and we should therefore follow ordained stipulations in order to move through life in a way that pleases God (Eccles. 8:7). Paul reflects on the problem of knowing in 1 Corinthians 13:12: "Now I know in part; then I shall know fully, even as I am fully known." Paul views our ability to know as limited until the consummation of the age.

In regard to knowing God's will, the impact of Adam's sin has distorted our ability to know the mind of God immediately and accurately. We lost our capacity to know God correctly on our own because our reasoning processes have been tainted (cf. 1 Cor. 2:6–16). The earth yields thistles; people distort the Creator. Salvation alone does not overcome this problem of distortion (cf. 1 Corinthians 1–3), because as 1 Corinthians 13:12 reminds us, we will only see clearly at the final consummation. (See figure 2.) When you try to look to God, you have to peer through layers of distortion brought about by the fall. Furthermore, your own capacity to think is tainted! Is there hope?

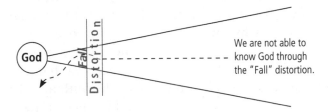

Fig. 2. The Dilemma of Knowing God

The Distortion Solution

First Corinthians 2:6–16 explains God's provision for overcoming the problem of knowing.[2] The first letter to the Corinthians is not friendly. An influential group within the Corinth church challenged Paul's representation of the gospel message. Paul wrote to them to explain the origin and authority of the message he proclaimed. Chapters 1–4 particularly address this problem, with 2:6–16 as the explanation of why the message of the cross is valid. Paul informs the Corinthians that the message he proclaims is not his own bright idea but divinely revealed truth. This truth is so special that it can only be known by accepting it as revealed truth (see 2:6–16; 14:37–38). Let's look at 1 Corinthians 2:6–16 in its context and see how Paul explained how he knew this message was from God and not his own invention.

Paul confronted a community that resisted his exposition of the gospel, a community eaten up with division and rivalry. In chapters 1–4, he presented an apology for his ministry and its message. He argued that his ministry was not for self-promotion but was focused on Christ (1:10–17). The message of the cross that Paul preached was based on God's wisdom, not Paul's. This message had an edge that some Corinthians wished to avoid (1:18–25). The Corinthians' initial conversion demonstrated the power of Paul's message (1:26–31), so why the change? Paul's approach modeled a message that stood on its own without power plays by the speaker (2:1–5). Although Paul's ministry was hampered by the factional and foolish values of the Corinthians (3:1–23), his ministry was confirmed as valid by its own testimony (4:1–21).

In the midst of the flow of chapters 1–4, 2:6–16 provides Paul's epistemology (how he knows what he knows!) for the message of the cross. Stop here and read this passage from your own Bible. Please note that the content of this passage reflects the biblical story we have described previously, rehearsing the dilemma of a fallen race that does not know God or his will. Verse 9 is the crescendo of 1 Corinthians 2:6–9:

"No eye has seen,
    no ear has heard,
no mind has conceived
    what God has prepared for those who love him"—

This verse has nothing to do with the promise of heaven, as it is often applied; rather it states the fact that the world cannot know God's will without help (the sentence ends with 2:10). The failure of the senses and unaided reason to know God's will for salvation leaves humanity in a major dilemma. The wisdom of Paul's message does not originate from human wisdom but from God. This wisdom is described as "hidden" (2:7) and the exclusive property of God. Verse 9 clearly states that the sense perception of "eye" and "ear" cannot provide the message. Neither can reason originate the divine will—"no mind has conceived." If we stopped with 2:9, we would forever be in darkness concerning who God is and what he requires of us. We cannot know these things without God's direct intervention to provide us with knowledge of himself and his ways.

In spite of our dilemma, 1 Corinthians 2:10 brings God's solution for the problem of knowledge into bold relief: "But God has revealed it [the message] to us [the apostles and through them to the rest of us] by his Spirit." The key term here is *revealed*. When the human race was at a loss to know God, God himself overcame that dilemma by direct revelation. Figure 2, describing our dilemma, now needs one additional perspective. God revealed himself and his will in the Bible (see figure 3). Divine revelation is the only way to bypass the distortion imposed on the world by sin. Paul speaks about how God's mind was communicated to humankind in 2:10–13. This section is the most detailed explanation of the process of revelation in the Bible. Yet this process is still hard to comprehend. Paul declares the fact of the process by analogies, but he does not explain it. Such a process cannot be put into a scientific test tube. We can accept Paul's affirmation and understand it, but we will never comprehend this Spirit-enacted process. In fact, that is exactly what 1 Corinthians 2:14–16 states!

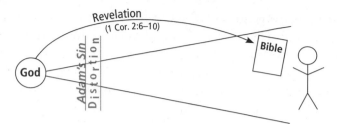

Fig. 3. God's Solution to the Dilemma

The product of revelation that Paul declares in 1 Corinthians is the Bible. Even though the Bible provides an accurate record of God's mind, we as readers still have the problem of our own mental distortion. The Bible becomes subject to imperfect interpretation, because interpretation is a human task. Consequently, the solution God has provided is only partial. God has not chosen to overcome the mental distortion we all possess. This is why we need the exhortation of Romans 12:1–2, to be transformed by the renewing of our minds.

The solution, therefore, to the problem of knowing, is that God overcomes our lack of knowing his mind by means of revelation. Yet, how does God reveal? When does God reveal? To whom does God reveal? Is a revealing act common property of all believers or something reserved for specially called persons? Is a revealing act normative for God's guidance of his children? How does the Bible portray God's revealing acts in regard to the direction of believers in life's decisions? We will discuss these questions as we proceed through the following chapters. For now, it is important to note that the problem of knowing God and his will requires that God communicate to us. We are not sufficient in ourselves to know God's mind without help. As we continue our study, we will develop the proposition that the Bible is God's sufficient communication to us to know his will, if we will only learn to read and apply its truths appropriately. We will also see that God's revealing acts are special and not normal operating procedure. God's recorded acts of revelation provide for us the data we need to pursue life's decisions. As with Adam, God defines our fences and expects us to tend the garden within his guidelines.

The Quest to Know God and His Will

The desire to know God has obstacles, both external and internal. Adam's sin affected the world we live in and the minds we use to interpret our world. Those who place their faith in the God of the Bible still struggle to know God in terms of his desires for how they should live life on earth. That quest has occupied the attention of believers through the ages. Our knowledge of God and his will depends upon his choice to disclose himself and his desires. We depend totally upon such self-disclosure in order to have accurate knowledge concerning our Creator and his will. A brief review of how the Bible records the quest of believers to know God and of how God has responded uncovers a pattern of God's method of revealing himself.

The term *knowledge* first appears in the Bible in Genesis 2:9: "the tree of the knowledge of good and evil." This tree is the central symbol of the Garden of Eden. It distinguished between God and humanity, between choosing a life of obedience to God's revealed will and choosing disobedience and death. God viewed Adam's violation of the tree as death (2:17). The serpent presented it as the gateway to becoming like God in the realm of knowledge (3:5). Eve interpreted it as "desirable for gaining wisdom" (3:6). For whatever reasons, Adam and Eve were not satisfied with God's provision of knowledge. They wanted to launch out on their own and become independent persons, capable of knowing by, and for, themselves. Their choice also carried them into a new realm of moral independence from God by breaking his command. Rejecting God's way of knowing was an act of open rebellion. The consequences of their actions included banishment from the Garden, the place symbolizing the presence of God and his open communication with his creation. This environment is now replaced with pain and only an occasional word from God.

Genesis 4–11 covers hundreds of years of earth history, with Noah as a bright spot in the midst of moral darkness. For a long period of time, God's communication to his creation seems meager. Then Abraham appears and Genesis 12–50 recounts the story of God's dealing with Abraham and his seed. This period covers a history of about 350 years. Abraham lived around 2000–1825 B.C.E., and Joseph died around 1640 B.C.E. No written Bible as we know it existed at this time. God's communication to his people came in occasional events represented by "the Lord said to . . ." Knowledge of God was conveyed to select individuals, such as Abraham, and they in turn conveyed it to others. Oral tradition of these communications from God was the source of knowledge at that time.

What we know as the Bible, particularly the Jewish Scriptures, began its written history as Scripture with Moses, around 1450 B.C.E. according to a prominent dating method. Job may be an early exception to this. Moses' knowledge of God was twofold. He received the oral tradition that had existed since Eden, and he received direct communication from God. The historical narrative of his writings probably utilized the existing traditions under the divine umbrella of inspired preservation. The law codes, however, were particularly a part of direct divine revelation (see Exodus 19 and 34). This was true of the core law codes and many other regulations. "The Lord said to Moses . . ." is a common introduction to sections in Exodus and

Leviticus. Deuteronomy, a title that means "second law," was chosen to symbolize Moses' rehearsal of the law to Israel in the wilderness. Moses had previously received and taught this material. As he repeated that original teaching, it seems Moses expanded the application of its values to new real-life situations. Although we cannot do this in an inspired manner as Moses did, the principle of applying biblical truth to life's situations is still our responsibility.

The first five books of the Bible, the Pentateuch, provide the theological foundations for the rest of the Old Testament, and even the New Testament. It is interesting to observe how the writings that follow Moses' writings reflected and built upon what he provided. God continues to give direct revelation from time to time, but the Pentateuch provided the core, and it was the responsibility of future generations to relate to it.

The psalmists reflected upon the law in relation to life (Psalms 1, 119), the writers of Proverbs used the law as a base for the development of wisdom (Prov. 3:1–6; 28:7), and the prophets were covenant policemen calling Israel back to obedience to the ancient laws that God had given them (Isa. 8:16, 20; 51:7; Jer. 26:4–6; Dan. 6:5). When we realize that the law reflects a relationship between God and Israel and is not just rules and regulations for its own end, the law becomes much more powerful to guide life, as the biblical writers so ably illustrated.

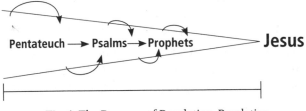

Pentateuch → Psalms → Prophets   **Jesus**

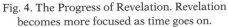

Fig. 4. The Progress of Revelation. Revelation becomes more focused as time goes on.

The pattern of each successive generation of believers living from the "deposit" received from God's past revelation is a major theme in Scripture (see figure 4). The basic ideas given in the core information of revelation become more focused throughout time. Old Testament writers such as the psalmists and prophets illustrate this pattern, as we have noted. The pattern continues with Jesus and the apostles. Jesus' incarnation and earthly ministry fulfilled the first phase of messianic promises of the Old Testament. During his earthly existence, Jesus ordered his life according to relevant Old Testament passages. During the wilderness temptation, Satan called the personhood and mission of Jesus into question. Jesus appealed exclusively to the Book of Deuteronomy to combat Satan's attacks (Matt. 4:1–11). Jesus, as the unique Son of God, was capable of bringing God's Word into existence in his own speech. He chose, however, to live his life on the basis of Old Testament teaching. Jesus commanded his apostles to continue this pattern by saying, "[Teach] them to obey everything I have commanded you" (Matt. 28:20).

Paul captured the continuation of this pattern of passing on revealed truth as the standard for living in his second letter to Timothy: "And the things you have heard me say in the presence of many witnesses entrust to reliable men who will also be qualified to teach others" (2 Tim. 2:2). The apostles and their protégés normally taught by passing on the "deposit" of truth revealed to the believing community by God's special means (Luke 1:1–4; 1 Cor. 15:1–5; 2 Peter 1:12–21; 3:15–16). Each successive generation of believers is responsible to live from the revelatory deposit of previous generations. God's acts of special revelation vary with each generation, but this pattern never varies within the biblical testimony. Each successive generation of believers draws their knowledge of God and his will primarily from the record of God's special revelatory acts.

Conclusion

In this chapter we have explored the problem of "knowing" and how the God of the Bible has addressed it for his followers. I am glad that God designed us with sense perception, the ability to reason, intuition, and authority. These ways of knowing bring our world alive. Yet we need help to know the mind of God. In the biblical story, the disobedience of Adam and Eve in the Garden of Eden plunged the human race into a dilemma. The heirs of Adam's sin do not naturally know God or his ways. Paul reminded us in 1 Corinthians 2:6–16 that even the most intelligent and powerful persons in society cannot construct an accurate understanding of God and his will. The only way to overcome our distorted understanding is for God to perform revelatory acts whereby he communicates accurate information about himself and his expectations for his creation. The most objective record of God's revelation is that which is contained in the Bible.

God addresses his children's quest to know him and his ways by placing his revealed will into a "deposit"-type reservoir so that each succeeding generation of believers can benefit from his self-disclosure. Finding guidance for life from this deposit, the Bible, is the normal way God guides his children. We will visit this idea in detail in part 2 as we survey the Bible and its "will of God" contexts.

When we understand the problem we face in knowing God and his will, we can begin to develop structures to help us reflect on what Jesus would really do if he were confronted with the same questions we face. Answers to our questions are not always found in a particular verse from the Bible but sometimes are found in understanding what the Bible teaches as a whole.[3] The first step in this development is to understand how to think within the framework of a biblical worldview and the values it provides. In the next chapter, you will learn what worldview-based thinking is all about.

2

The Need for a
Transformed Mind

■ Remember Mr. Spock of *Star Trek*? His pure logic approach bothered many of his colleagues, especially Dr. McCoy, who preferred more feeling in one's analysis of situations. One of Spock's abilities was the Vulcan mind meld. When Spock placed his fingers in the right place on another person's head and concentrated, he could move data from that person's mind to his. It would be nice to read another person's mind from time to time, wouldn't it? It would be even better if we could read the mind of God.

Yet the mind of God is available within the Bible he has given us (1 Cor. 2:16). When Romans 12:1–2 calls for every believer to have a "transformed mind," it exhorts us to learn to think God's way. Would it not be convenient if God would do something similar to Spock in order to transform our minds? At conversion, God could program us with "live godly" software! Or perhaps God could give us the capability to read his mind if we would just concentrate hard enough. Although conversion does change us, we know all too well that we still struggle to do what is right. And in certain circumstances, we struggle with knowing what to do! Where is our all-powerful God in all of this? Why has he chosen to leave us with such tensions?

The reality of life's struggle that we experience as Christians teaches us that God has not chosen any shortcuts for our moral and personal development. He created us to make choices and thereby glorify God by our thoughts and actions. The Garden of Eden illustrates that Adam and Eve were not moral robots, programmed to do only the will of God. The implication is clear that God wanted them to choose to do right. He wanted them to process decisions and choose the right path. They were responsible for their thoughts and actions. This is all part of being created in the image of God. We are thinking, choosing, self-determining, feeling, moral beings. God's design is that we seek him and his ways by our own choices. Therefore, in divine wisdom, as he gave Adam instructions in Eden, so he has given us instructions in his Word, the Bible. We glorify God by engaging that Word in our daily decision making.

Using the Lamp, Walking the Path

God could have done the Vulcan mind meld. Instead, God chose a path similar to that which every parent faces. He set the boundaries and within those parameters created an environment in which his children must pursue a decision-making process that reflects their created capacities. When we do this, God is glorified because his image is reflected in us. We would choose an easier and more direct route, one without risk and struggle. But our all-wise

Creator had a greater, although more complicated, plan to develop us as human beings.

The Romans 12 Factor

God provided the Bible to enable us to deal with the dilemma of knowing him and his ways. This provision, however, only provides a light for our path. We have to use the lamp and do the walk. God's solution only provides us with a database. We must learn to apply it to our situations in life, which is why we are commanded, "Be transformed by the renewing of your mind." We need to learn to think biblically.

THE CONTEXT AND IMPLICATIONS OF ROMANS 12:1–2

The Roman Empire controlled the world of Paul's time. The city of Rome was its governmental center. Paul was the apostle to the Gentiles, and Rome was a strategic city to evangelize and teach the ways of Christ. The Christian mission had already made inroads among the residents of Rome, but Paul had not yet been able to go to Rome to share his teaching about Christ. Since he could not be physically present, he wrote the Book of Romans to share the Christian message and encourage the believers in Rome (Rom. 1:8–13). Christians can be forever grateful for the circumstances that brought the Book of Romans into existence. Since Paul could not deliver his message orally, he wrote one of the most complete and theologically structured books of the New Testament.

Paul progressively moves through the major tenets of the Christian faith in Romans 1–8. He treats the themes of sin, righteousness, justification, salvation, the benefits and struggles of the believer's life, and the work of the Spirit of God in bringing God's plan to fulfillment in this life and in the life to come.

These early chapters make it clear that Christianity is rooted in the faith and belief structures of Abraham. Paul clarifies in Romans 9–11 the difficult issue some Jews had with God's calling of Paul to incorporate the Gentiles more significantly into God's plan. Jesus illustrated in Luke 4:14–30 that when the Jewish nation failed to respond to God, he raised up Gentiles who would hear and obey. Jesus' audience got the message and endeavored to kill him because of it (4:28–30).

Having established the theological foundations of the Christian faith in Romans 1–11, Paul turns to the application of belief in Romans 12–16. All of Paul's Epistles are organized by the twofold themes of theology and ethics (the application of theology). Paul always moves from right belief to right behavior, recognizing that behavior is the product of our thought patterns.

Romans 12:1–2 provides a hinge for the flow of the book. It states the expected results of the truth of chapters 1–11, "therefore," and leads the reader into an elaboration of ethics in chapters 12–16. The call to Christian commitment of Romans 12:1–2 is based on the believer's obligation to respond to God's grace as represented in the theological story of chapters 1–11. The language Paul used in this exhortation is drawn from Old Testament religious ceremony. In the Old Testament a sacrifice was brought to the altar to die so that the supplicant might have life and access to God. In Romans, we are "living sacrifices," since Christ already died for us. Our part of this process is to change the way we think, based on the analogy that we have died to the old ways and are now to live for the new values that come with salvation.

The fact that we need a transformed mind confirms the problem discussed in chapter 1 of this book, and assumes that we cannot know things correctly. We need help. Paul's statement also depends upon God revealing what is to be believed. The mind is not renewed in a vacuum. The renewal process depends on the presence of revealed truths, which the mind processes in order to change. These truths are the deposit that we find in the Bible, a book being composed during Paul's time. When Paul commanded that the Romans be transformed by the renewal of their minds, he did not leave them in a vacuum to figure out what needed to be renewed. He immediately began in verse 3 to teach them some of the life issues they needed to address.

Your Mind Matters: The Components of a Transformed Mind

Paul asserts that the renewed mind is required in order for the believer to "test and approve what God's will is" (Rom. 12:2). This statement places a great deal of responsibility on the believer to pursue a process of discernment. It certainly does not promote a subjective process as the way to find God's will. We "approve" what is the "good, pleasing and perfect will" by evaluating life from the perspective of a transformed mind.

What are the components in this process? The two primary components are our own mind and will. We must grow in our ability to think biblically about our decisions and then exercise the will to do so. Consider the mental framework first.

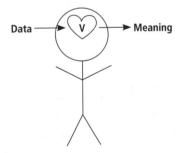

Fig. 5. The Transformed Mind

The mechanics of how the mind interprets data are the same for all human beings (see figure 5). When we are confronted with data, it is first filtered through the mind, where we evaluate it in light of the worldview and values that control our thinking processes. This process assigns meaning to the data in keeping with that worldview and values set. In figure 5, the mind is depicted by a heart symbol, because people in biblical times viewed thinking in relation to the heart (Matt. 5:28; 15:19; Luke 2:19, 51; Rom. 10:9–10). The V within the mind stands for the values we hold. The illustration depicts the data moving through the mind, which ascribes it meaning. Although God assigned meaning to all reality in creation, human beings still interpret their world according to their own thinking processes. The purpose of a transformed mind is to grow to interpret our world in conformity with God's view.

Let me illustrate how this mental process works. We have two persons, Mrs. X and Mrs. Y. Mrs. X is a Christian and Mrs. Y is an atheist. Each of these persons is presented the data "sin." The word *sin* is run through the filters/minds of each of these women. Mrs. X is an educated Presbyterian and she assigns *sin* the following meaning: "a transgression of the righteous law of God, and contrary thereunto, does in its own nature, bring guilt upon the sinner, whereby he is bound over to the wrath of God, and curse of the law, and so made subject to death, with all miseries spiritual, temporal, and eternal."[1] On the other hand, Mrs. Y assigns a very different meaning. She is well educated and knows that *sin* is a religious term, but she rejects how religious documents define this word. She asserts that sin merely means that a person has broken a social code as some group has defined it. Mrs. Y has no ultimate concept of sin, because she rejects the idea of an eternal God to whom humans must give an account.

For Mrs. Y, all ideas of sin are socially constructed and therefore subject to various definitions and applications. What is a sin for one person, according to Mrs. Y, may not be a sin for another person. After all, there are "different strokes for different folks."

What causes such a radical difference between these two women? Is it the word *sin?* No. "Sin" is merely a phonetic symbol to which they assign meaning. The difference between Mrs. X and Y lies in their minds. They think differently about this term and therefore assign different meanings to it. Mrs. X used to think like Mrs. Y, but she became a Christian and adopted a new view of sin.

Human beings assign meaning to data on the basis of the way they think about life. We call this a worldview and values set.

Let's apply another situation to Mrs. X and Y. Assume that each of these ladies was confronted with an appealing opportunity to commit adultery. Mrs. X feels the temptation but refuses to yield because this would violate the clear teaching of the Bible about sexual relationships and also her personal values about the husband and family she loves. Mrs. Y also experiences a real draw to commit adultery. She also refuses to do so. She does not refuse, however, because of biblical values. She doesn't believe they are binding on her. She refuses because she values her husband and children and will not break that trust. In this situation, both ladies make the same decision for similar reasons. Mrs. X, however, also claims that her values are biblically derived and therefore ultimately the correct values.

The Bible repeatedly teaches that as a person thinks, he or she acts. Our behavior is never an accident. We are responsible for our actions. The key is to engage the process of that responsibility in a reflective manner so that we take control of our decisions rather than become their victims.

The mental framework of the transformed mind is common to all human beings. Paul called for Christians to change the way they interpret their world by changing the way they think. We need to think like Christians. We need to adjust our mental filters so that they operate from a biblical worldview and values set. That is a transformed mind. We are responsible to adjust the way we evaluate life and its issues so that we can make decisions in keeping with biblical teaching.

The second component of the transformed mind is the will. It is possible to know what is right or appropriate yet lack the determination to do it. Knowledge is not an end within itself; it is a means to an end. Mrs. X and Y could have made different decisions when confronted with an opportunity for adultery, but they chose (exercised their will) to maintain conformity of behavior with their views of life.

In summary, the renewal of our minds in the direction of biblical values transforms our behavior because it changes the way we think about life. We educate our values system to conform to the values presented in the Bible. This process provides us not only with clear moral commands but also with patterns of thinking. We begin to think of the good of a community rather than merely advancing our own agendas (Rom. 12:3–13; 14:1–15:13; Phil. 1:27–2:4). We learn to discipline our responses to people who would take advantage of us, indeed even to look out for their good rather than our own (Rom. 12:14–21)! We come to realize that we have worldly obligations, and we must recognize even those structures that are controlled by unbelievers, for they are created by God and are to be respected (Rom. 13:1–7).

Knowing and doing God's will is a process of learning to evaluate life from the perspective of divine values. It is not a search for a proof text for each decision or some extrabiblical subjective confirmation to point us in the right direction. Knowing and doing God's will requires that we develop the capacity to evaluate life's decisions from a biblical worldview and values system. We will not always have a proof text to address our questions, but we will always have a theological context from which to define our courses of action. The full sufficiency of the Bible for faith and practice comes to life when we understand how to think reflectively based on the totality of Scripture.

Developing a Christian Worldview and Value Complex

What Is a Worldview?

Before we examine the exhortation of Romans 12:1–2 to be transformed by the renewing of our minds, we must consider the structures of worldview and values as the arena where we make decisions about life's issues.

A worldview is the mental framework, or conceptual system, that gives meaning to all the components of our world and us. A worldview is the lens through which we see our world. Many different lenses have been proposed. Once you determine which lens to use, the whole world will appear as that lens color makes it. The atheist, evolutionist, humanist, polytheist, or Christian theist views and explains the world through his or her lens. An evolutionist looks at the galaxy and sees the "big bang." A Christian sees the product of the creative hand of God. Although each has elaborate reasons for his or her belief in how the world came to be, neither was present when creation occurred. Therefore, neither can fully explain reality without the framework they have chosen to apply. Both, however, have committed themselves to a set of presuppositions that give meaning to the data they evaluate. These presuppositions constitute a mental framework that becomes a set of beliefs about themselves and their world.[2]

Our worldview is at the center of our opinions about every issue of life (see figure 6).[3] This filter makes judgments about religion, what constitutes a family, how to relate to the environment, what is appropriate health care, what are human rights, what kind of education society should promote. People reach different conclusions about these issues, because their worldviews and values differ. Even committed Christians who appeal to the same Bible may view some issues differently. The key to decision making is identifying the reasons why we hold our views and explaining why we make our decisions.

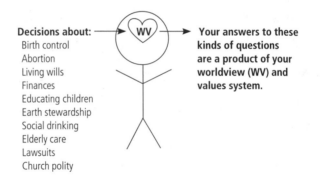

Fig. 6. The Organizing Worldview and Values Set

Through the lenses of our worldview we make judgments about who we are, how we know what we know, and what values drive our lives. These three items are the classic philosophical categories of *ontology* (being), *epistemology* (knowing), and *axiology* (doing/values). Serious life decisions about such issues as abortion, euthanasia, a living will, whom we marry, how we deal with financial debt, or what causes we support with our time and money are all informed by our views of personhood and how we understand biblical teaching. In chapter 1 we discussed the biblical story of creation, fall, redemption, and consummation. These categories are the core of a biblical worldview. The Bible's story of creation tells us about the origin of our world and ourselves. We understand personhood; the roles of women, men, children; and all manner of social relationships from the pages of Scripture. The fall gives us a rationale for our personal and global problems. We know that we live on a globe where bad things often happen to good and godly people. It is a fallen world with an environment and people who do not seek to serve the dictates of their Creator. But redemption gives us hope, and the consummation guarantees an ultimate purpose and direction in our world.

We all operate from a worldview regardless of our level of self-awareness about what guides our choices in life. A Christian worldview about life and death is why many in the church disagree with Dr. Kevorkian, who pressed the issue of euthanasia during the 1990s by performing numerous assisted suicides. He viewed his actions as humane. He and others could certainly list the practical reasons why choosing death would benefit the person and family who suffer toward an inevitable conclusion. But many, including Christians, the courts, and other religions, consider his actions to usurp not only the natural events of life but also the teaching of many religious traditions and the laws guiding our society. Dr. Kevorkian, Christians, other religions, and the courts were all informed by the worldview systems that guided their decisions.

September 11, 2001, brought into clear view two major worldviews: freedom-loving Americans and Islamic terrorists. We have observed that no amount of reasoning or appeal to what we view as human decency will dent the mindset of a terrorist and his commitment to his ideals. There is no ground for discussion, because these two worldviews are too radically opposed for dialogue. Islamic extremists view the American mindset, and its expansion around a globe that is becoming increasingly small, as undermining their culture. What is worse, their culture is their religion. Fanaticism in the name of religion is always the fiercest, because it claims to operate from eternal verities, yet clearly illustrates that a worldview drives human behavior.

What Are Values?

The Greek term for "worth/worthy," and therefore "of value," is *axios*. So axiology is the philosophical study of what we view as worthy or valuable. As you might imagine, axiology is a vast subject covering everything that deals with aesthetics (what is beauty) and ethics (moral values). We will only look at the idea of values as it serves how we categorize the decisions that we make.

For the purposes of a decision-making model, values are personal beliefs that guide our thinking and actions. Values are derived from our worldview. For example, the ultimate belief of a Christian is that God exists, he has communicated to us, and the Bible is the accurate record of that communication. This is at the core of our worldview. Given this fact, it should not surprise us that the Bible and its teaching becomes the core source for the development of our value system, controlling all our subsequent established values. On the basis of biblical teaching, we value love over hate, eternity over the brevity of life, honesty over dishonesty, faithfulness over infidelity, filial and social relationships over private interests, kindness over rudeness, faith over fear, giving over selfishness, personal hurt over revenge, and truth over error. We place the grid of biblical teaching over every decision we make and thereby justify our thinking and actions in a way that conforms to the truth God has revealed.

Few Christians have a problem discerning the clear commands of God contained in the Bible. You are reading this book, however, because you desire help in discerning God's will for your life when there does not seem to be a clear command applying to your situation. You are tempted to question whether the Bible really is sufficient for your life. But the real life you experience illustrates why you must learn to think from a biblical values perspective. Most of our decisions require us to think in larger categories than the direct command structure of the Bible. For example, where do you go in the Bible to address the situation of an abused spouse? No simple proof text addresses this burning issue in our current culture. Discerning God's will in order to help individuals caught in a cycle of violence requires us to apply larger biblical categories to our questions. What is the value of a person? Why should one person value another person? If one truly values another, how does that affect how he or she treats another person? If a person's life is valuable, what measures should be taken to protect her from physical harm? God's will is found in answering biblically the many questions attending any issue you confront. If you revert to a prayer such as, "God show me what to do with this situation," and do not do your homework in the Bible, you have abrogated your responsibility to the revealed will of God.

We must think from a biblical worldview and values level, with mature reflection about God, our world, and ourselves. We know by experience that this kind of thinking is necessary. We see from Romans 12:1–2 that it is expected of us; but most Christians find it hard to think this way. What the Bible provides, when used to its full extent, is much bigger and better than most Christians have ever experienced. Most are locked into the small scenario of looking for words in the Bible to confirm their actions rather than qualifying those actions by the larger category of biblical values. The Bible is misused if we make it into a spiritual Ouija board to magically discern life rather than seeing it as a record of God's dealings with his people from which we derive truth and values for living. We will return to this crucial issue, but for the moment let us consider the various levels of values we should understand and develop.

Three levels of values are constant in life's decisions: clear biblical commands, community values, and our personal preferences that reflect who we are in our calling and giftedness from God. Sitting down to a meal in a restaurant that serves alcoholic beverages may bring all three levels of values into play as we order our meal. We are immediately processing what we know about biblical teaching about wine. We are reflecting upon what our worshiping community thinks about this issue. And we are interfacing our own preferences pro or con with the two preceding levels. Our response to the waitress may be given with a sense of freedom, because we believe the Bible allows wine as a beverage when used in moderation and our worshiping community understands and allows the exercise of this freedom. Or we might say no to the waitress because we value a community with which we associate that asks us to suspend such a practice. In this case, we suspend what we believe is a right in order to honor a group with which we want to associate. Happy is the Christian who can deal with such issues on the basis of knowledge rather than manipulation. How we respond to such situations, and more importantly, how we explain our response, exposes our biblical knowledge and how we apply our values in the real world.

The *first level* of development for the transformed mind relates to biblical commands. For example, "Do not forni-cate or commit adultery" is not open to debate. It is a clear command of God in both testaments and is immediately understood by all. Jesus gives such commands an internal meaning that exposes our values. External sexual com-mands often protect the powerless in social relationships and thereby highlight the value of respecting personhood. But not all biblical commands are as apparent. For exam-ple, what does it mean to "love God"? No believer debates this requirement, but can you explain what it means? The meaning of "love your neighbor as yourself" is more chal-lenging. This great commandment, "to love God and your neighbor," was actually developed to summarize the many aspects of the Mosaic Law. Love became a supreme value that guided the understanding and application of legal stipulations.

A *second level* of values development relates to what I call "community values." Every group establishes a values system that it expects its members to observe. Christianity is quite complex in this regard. The community values of any Christian group usually claim lines of continuity with level-one values (biblical commands). The reasons behind such values, however, are often a matter of debate between or within communities. The Bible does not pro-vide proof texts for what constitutes good music, but

Christian communities often have opinions about this
and may claim that their views best promote texts that
call for purity of mind. By doing this, a clear biblical value
is taken and applied to a debated issue. But this is part of
the nature of values, since they are often abstract rather
than concrete. Community values may also go the second
mile in order to be a witness to the local world in which
they operate. The community may know that the Bible
does not prohibit the use of wine, but they may choose to
practice abstinence for their view of testimony. How one
understands biblical commands and extends them into
values often brings conflict to a community, as it did in
Corinth during Paul's time (1 Corinthians 8–10; see also
Romans 12–14).

As I write this material, a respected Reformed Church
of America college in our area is in the news. Its hockey
team is anticipating a national championship game. The
final game, however, is scheduled for a Sunday. The institution practices a strict "Christian Sabbath" policy, excluding
sports teams from playing on Sunday. They have announced
that they will forfeit this game if it occurs on Sunday. For
some this may seem like a severe example, but it is real in
certain religious communities.

A *third level* of values is constituted by each individual's personal preferences. Many of our preferences
are the product of our entire lives and contain no
moral overtones. I hold chocolate ice cream to be of
more value than vanilla! I was raised in Midwest farm
country and still like my meat and potatoes. I have also
revised some eating values in light of health and age!
Our pursuit of a transformed mind may also affect our
personal values. I never valued reading, public speaking, or advanced education until I became a Christian.
I have come to value time with people more than I used

to. I believe these changes are in keeping with biblical values.

Both community and personal values are subject to the control of direct command values. As we grow in our understanding of what the Bible actually teaches, community and personal values are usually revised to match that understanding. Such revision may be more restrictive or more relaxed. I often watch churches and individual Christians struggle with such change. Sometimes communities or individuals may deify their values, or the traditions from which many of their values are drawn, in such a way that growth in understanding and consequent change becomes very difficult. How a church relates to the rising number of "singles again" (note even the euphemism for death or divorce) may illustrate how values have changed (or become better focused, depending on your viewpoint) over the last couple of decades. Communities or persons who do not experience change in how they evaluate life's decisions are stagnant in terms of the renewal of their minds. Growth in our understanding of the Bible and God's ways never ends.

Getting in touch with our worldview and values set is crucial in our quest to discern God's will for our lives. God has ordained a process of mental renewal as the foundation to discerning his will (Rom. 12:1–2). This is not a mystical will of God that we must find in order to know what to do. Rather, it is the biblical idea of God's will. Knowing and doing God's will in the Bible is knowing and obeying his teaching. This teaching is not only the clear direct commands, but also the worldview and values set derived from the whole presentation of the Bible. God has fulfilled his part of the process by giving us his Word. We must assimilate that Word so that we may reflect God in the decisions we make.

In the later chapters of this book, we will view how the Old and New Testaments reflect the will of God as the fulfillment of God's teaching.

Dealing with Christian Diversity

Have you ever thought, *Why do Christians, who all claim the same Bible as their authority, not exhibit unity of belief and values? Why do different church communities interpret the same Bible verse with very different results? Why has God not imposed a unity of belief and values on the church?* These are big questions and yield no simple answers. But the questions indicate that God has ordained a process whereby we are responsible to deal with our world and God's revealed precepts in order to make judgments. For whatever reason, God has not chosen to impose total unity upon our conclusions. Although there may be only one right answer to a question, God may suspend imposing that answer to achieve other purposes in our moral and spiritual development. We are all too familiar with the diversity of views about church governance, baptism, the Lord's Supper (Eucharist), and the millennium, to name only a few. Remember, we have an inspired Bible but no inspired commentaries!

God has decreed a process that includes a degree of risk and struggle for his creation. God could have micro-managed every decision we make, but he chose not to. I believe the real world we experience is part of God's grand plan to display us as created in his image. Without risk and struggle, we would never grow as image bearers. As a parent creates an environment in which children can mature, so God has ordained our journey to conform us to the image of his own dear Son. This theme will be revisited from time to time as we see this model of God's dealing with us arise within the biblical record.

Conclusion

We have presented several major themes from the biblical story about knowing God and his will. Scripture teaches us that we cannot know God or his will without divine revelation. Once God has revealed his will, the record of this information provides the means whereby the followers of God can discern the desires of God for his creation. We are responsible to acquire an understanding of God and his ways from the biblical record and thereby be transformed by the renewing of our minds. We are then enabled to interpret the decisions of life from a values base in keeping with God's revealed will.

The challenges we experience in knowing God's will are seldom in the area of God's direct commands. The clear commands of Scripture need merely to be obeyed. The difficulty of discernment relates to all the areas where there is no direct Bible verse to address our question. Our questions, however, are still addressed by the Bible, within its worldview structure. The ability to think within a biblical worldview and values structure is the key to making decisions that please God.

The next chapter will present a model for processing decisions. This "big picture" presentation will set the stage for the remaining chapters of this book.

A Preview of a Worldview and Values Model

■ A close Christian friend of mine, Jean, was put in charge of spending six figures to equip an outpatient surgery center with computer equipment. She was the office manager and seemed to be the one in the office who knew the most about computers. She was petrified. The whole office was computer challenged and she was barely ahead of the pack. Furthermore, she knew some programs but not the hardware side of computer systems.

Jean did her job and researched several vendors. She narrowed it down to two. One vendor, based in Indianapolis, represented a well-known computer company. The other was a new vendor in Lebanon, Indiana. The Indianapolis rep was "Mr. Clean." He had all the answers about hardware and a big name to provide service. But his software package was not exactly what Jean's office needed, although it would work. The rep from Lebanon was a computer geek who looked like he had just crawled out of a suitcase! He also had all the answers, and he had a new medical software program that was customized to Jean's office needs. His product was the best choice by Jean's research, but she was scared to choose this new firm over the well-known company and wondered if this strange fellow could deliver on his promises. Thousands of dollars were at stake. A busy practice needed good and timely service. Could the Lebanon company provide this?

Jean had reached the midnight hour of decision and was torn between an established reputation and a newcomer. On the day of decision, Jean was home at lunch reading her Bible and praying for a divine answer to this dilemma. Lo and behold, when she opened her Bible, her eye fell on Jeremiah 22:20. All she saw was "Go up to Lebanon . . ."! She just about went through the ceiling! She knew my opinion about using the Bible like an Ouija board. She came to my office with Bible in hand and said, "Okay, explain this one to me!"

My answer began by reviewing with Jean her research and the conclusions she had drawn. She was convinced that Lebanon was the choice, but she was afraid. I told her to go with her research. I didn't tell her that the context of Jeremiah 22 related to God using the prophet to condemn Lebanon for her false sense of security (v. 21) or that the reference to Lebanon was a negative example of God's pending wrath (vv. 22–23)! I didn't give her my paraphrase of verse 20: "Woe to those who go up to Lebanon for help"!

I can fully enjoy a moment of mystery such as Jean experienced, but I cannot build a model of decision making upon it as some do. To do so would be to condone an irresponsible use of the Bible. A biblical process of discernment cannot be built on a procedure that is little more than

Christian divination and pagan in its origin and method. We cannot violate what the Bible intends to teach simply because we have a rare experience we cannot explain. God has designed a better way, one that drives us deep into the Bible and places a great deal of responsibility on us. It is a way that maturates us toward the transformed mind of Romans 12.

"The person who fails to plan, plans to fail." Most of us have violated this well-known cliché from time to time! Decision making requires planned reflection. We must first clearly identify and define the issues about which we must make a decision. Then we need to process the questions that surface in this procedure through our mental filter. This filter/grid enables us to evaluate issues in light of the worldview and values set we have acquired up to that point in time. In order to pursue this process, we need a clear understanding of how to visualize it. My chart in the next section attempts to help you do this.

In parts 2 and 3 we will visit the biblical texts and argue that this model represents the normal way God has designed for us to process the decisions of life.

Seeing the Big Picture

The chart in figure 7 will help us to think through a process of Christian decision making. It illustrates the process that our mind should go through as it evaluates the issues we confront. No illustration can be comprehensive, but this chart provides a framework that you can utilize and expand. The rectangular boxes represent the points where you evaluate questions, and the arrows show the flow of this process. All of this and more goes on inside your mind every day of your life. The real question is whether you are conscious of how you make judgments.

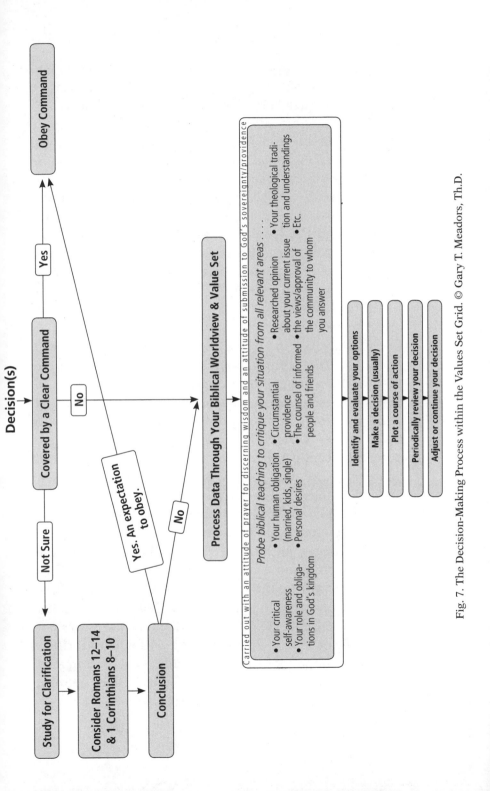

Decision(s)

Covered by a Clear Command

Yes → Obey Command

Not Sure → Study for Clarification → Consider Romans 12–14 & 1 Corinthians 8–10 → Conclusion

Yes. An expectation to obey. → Obey Command

No → Conclusion

No → Process Data Through Your Biblical Worldview & Value Set

Carried out with an attitude of prayer for discerning wisdom and an attitude of submission to God's sovereignty/providence

Probe biblical teaching to critique your situation from all relevant areas . . . .

- Your critical self-awareness
- Your role and obligations in God's kingdom
- Your human obligation (married, kids, single)
- Personal desires
- Circumstantial providence
- The counsel of informed people and friends
- Researched opinion about your current issue
- the views/approval of the community to whom you answer
- Your theological tradition and understandings
- Etc.

Identify and evaluate your options

Make a decision (usually)

Plot a course of action

Periodically review your decision

Adjust or continue your decision

Fig. 7. The Decision-Making Process within the Values Set Grid. © Gary T. Meadors, Th.D.

The pursuit of God's will is simply a process of evaluating life's questions in light of the worldview and values that we recognize and apply. Please read the rest of this section with constant reference to the decision-making chart. The first question highlighted in the chart requires that we clarify whether we are dealing with a clear command or directive that the Bible has already explicitly provided. If we are, then we need to obey the truth we already know. If we are not sure, then we need to clarify the nature of the issue confronting us. The "weak" and "strong" brother sections of Romans and 1 Corinthians illustrate how nonmoral issues can become moral issues if not treated appropriately.

Although the contexts of 1 Corinthians and Romans are different, they contain some common themes about God's will. First, the worldview of the weak was wrong and that of the strong was right. Second, the strong were to take the responsibility to create an environment in which the weak could have space to deal with their wrong understandings in an appropriate manner. Those who had a proper worldview could, however, morally violate other believers if they forced them to violate their convictions before they had an opportunity to adjust their understandings (decision-making grids). Romans 14:20–21 and 1 Corinthians 8:11–12 warn the strong not to abuse the weak by forcing them to mature faster than they are able. To do so is sin (1 Cor. 8:12). In these contexts, the value of community is higher than personal rights. This is a unique value in the Christian worldview. At the same time, do not forget that Paul did not accommodate the views of the weak. He publicly stated that they were not right while making it clear that there are higher priorities. He did not intend for the weak to rule the world. In fact, I think we can assume that if the weak do not change, they may eventually be dealt with as belligerent rather than weak.

Analogies to these first-century circumstances in our current settings are not easily identified, but we need to think about possible parallels. The pagan temple influence on the meat in the market may not be on the mind of a Western Christian, but I have had students from Asia who confront this in their churches. The issue of wine (Rom. 14:21) could be a parallel in the American church. How believers deal with Sunday practices might be an issue in some churches. This part of our chart certainly calls for higher-level thinking than simple obedience to clear commands.

If we conclude that we have a situation that is not addressed by a specific passage in the Bible, or the model of Romans and 1 Corinthians, then we proceed to a more elaborate process of analysis that will help us think about how the Bible does address our question (the big box in the chart).

While the entire chart represents our mental process, the large box brings the transformed mind of Romans 12 into focus. When an issue presents itself for evaluation, we need first to identify the categories that relate to the issue under review. For example, if a decision is to buy a home or rent, what questions should we review for this issue? Such a decision would at the least relate to values pertaining to family, finances, and geography of life circumstances. When we identify the categories, we begin to probe the Bible for the values that relate to the category. For example, the Bible generally teaches us to live within our means so that we can meet our financial obligations. If our resources dictate that we can afford a $150,000 home, we should not look at $250,000 homes. We should reflect on our own consciousness for what values motivate us to make a decision.

Are we motivated by need or desires to "keep up with the Joneses"? Or perhaps we value investment over paying a landlord. Do we exhibit patience or impatience about our life status? What value do we place on debt or no debt? In fact, what is our view of debt? Should we make a long-term commitment to our present geographical location? These are just a few general observations about the question as we endeavor to interface it with our already established values system.

The categories in the large box at the bottom of the chart represent a few basic biblical categories that help us analyze life's decisions. Each category has its own set of values. These values may vary between people and may change over time. However, they reflect common issues that each of us must address. For example, a common area with numerous values but which changes as our circumstances change is that of human obligations. Are we single or married, or married with kids, or married with aging parents? Each of these categories brings with it multiple biblical texts and expectations.

A former student of mine, Mark, was in our home recently for dinner. Mark has been in our home as a single, married, and married with a child. I have watched his view of life and sense of changing obligations develop over the last few years. He commented during his last visit that he never could have predicted how having a child would reorganize his priorities and view of life. There are good biblical reasons for these changes and the values that accompany them. Our status in terms of single, married, or family brings with it certain biblically defined obligations and parameters that influence how we respond to life's events.

All of the items in this box, and the many others we could create, can be developed theologically and thereby yield certain obligations and values taught by the Bible. Our growing understanding of what the Bible teaches in these various areas molds how we analyze life's issues. The clarification of biblical teaching and values is the larger process that Paul exhorts in Romans 12. We are responsible to deal with life as Christians. God has given us his Word and expects us to use it in our everyday living. This process helps us ask the right questions in relation to the decisions we face. When we learn to use questions to draw appropriate meaning from Scripture, we often find the answers we seek.

We will address the categories of this chart in greater detail in chapter 7, but let me now explain how values influenced one person in biblical history.

How to Live a Miserable Life!

The Old Testament character Lot, the nephew of Abraham, provides an interesting illustration of how a value-driven model operates in decision making. I believe Lot had the right values, but he made all the wrong choices. The incidents involving Abraham and Lot in Genesis 12–19 occurred around 2000 B.C.E., although Moses did not provide the biblical record until around 1450 B.C.E. Abraham knew God by direct revelation and oral tradition long before what we know as the Bible was produced. What Lot knew about God, he most likely learned directly from Abraham.

The Genesis account depicts Lot leaving Mesopotamia with Abraham and becoming an apprentice in husbandry with Abraham (12:4; 13:1, 5). In due time, Lot's herds became large enough to cause conflict with Abraham's growing flock. Abraham recognized this problem and took the initiative to solve it by giving Lot the first choice in claiming a territory (Gen. 13:5–9). Lot made a choice that was best for his herds. He occupied the well-watered area of Sodom and Gomorrah. The writer of Genesis makes it clear editorially that this was a choice that violated good judgment (13:12–13). Genesis 13:14–17 implies that Lot's choice not only separated him from Abraham but also from the divine blessing that God provided Abraham. Lot placed himself outside the ongoing flow of God's self-revelation and instruction. Lot's subsequent behavior and choices may reflect the kind of value conflict that led him to Sodom in the first place.

Although Lot was geographically on his own, the story portrays that Abraham was still his nephew's keeper (Genesis 14; 18:16–33). The classic illustration of Abraham's endeavor to care for Lot is the account of God communicating to Abraham his decision to destroy Sodom and Gomorrah. This gave Abraham the opportunity to intercede for Lot and his family, an opportunity he quickly pursued (18:22–33). When the two angels arrived at Sodom, Lot is found to be an entrenched resident of the city and an official in its judicial system (indicated by the phrase "in the gate" of 19:1). Lot's initiative with these visitors indicates his nervousness about their safety in the city in light of Sodom's moral climate, an implication that is confirmed in the events of the evening. When the visitors reveal God's coming judgment and Lot's opportunity to deliver his family, Lot is unable to influence his future sons-in-law to flee. The next morning Lot, his wife, and two daughters escape the destruction of the city. His wife's sympathy for Sodom and her apparent anger with God about the event cost her life. To make matters worse, in the aftermath of the destruction, Lot's daughters committed incest with their father and brought forth two sons whose progeny became the nations of Moab and Ammon. Lot fades from the historical record, although his acts live on in infamy within the biblical record and Jewish history.[1]

The Genesis account of Lot's sojourn in Sodom comes alive in the interpretive comments of 2 Peter 2:4–9. Peter's reference to Lot peers into the internal reflections of Lot as he lived in the Sodom environment. Let's examine verses 7–8.

> . . . and if he rescued Lot, a righteous man, who was distressed by the filthy lives of lawless men (for that righteous man, living among them day after day, was tormented in his righteous soul by the lawless deeds he saw and heard)—

Peter gives us several insights into Lot's life. He repeatedly refers to Lot as "righteous." *Righteous* in the Bible usually refers to "do right" behavior—for example, conformity to God's commands. Paul also images righteousness as the forensic state of being saved, our status with God. The Genesis account does not portray Lot as one who made good choices. In fact, he even became an example of a notorious sinner in early Jewish literature. Perhaps Peter emphasized Lot's status before God because we would not have given Lot such credit by what we know. Calling him "righteous" and referring to the behavior of Sodom as "lawless" sets a context of standards and values. The distress and torment of Lot's inner being was due to his living in an environment that violated the truth and values he had learned from Abraham.

Peter's use of "distressed" and "tormented" depicts a person who was in serious mental conflict in the realm of values. *Distressed* is the translation of a Greek word that means "to cause distress through oppressive means, subdue, torment, wear out, oppress."[2] This type of oppression is inflicted by someone onto someone. In Genesis, Lot is oppressed by the deviant values of the inhabitants of

Sodom. This oppression is reflected in Genesis 19:9 when the Sodomites became angry that Lot would dare to voice his judgment about their actions. This is a bright spot in the Lot narrative, although the offer of his virgin daughters is uttered almost in the same breath!

The second term, *tormented*, translates a Greek word that means to subject one to harassment. It is a severe term that is also used to reflect torture and punitive judicial procedures sometimes applied to slaves in antiquity.[3] Peter depicts Lot as subjecting himself to continuous inner torment by living in the midst of Sodom (2 Peter 2:8). This is amplified when one remembers that Lot sat with the city elders "in the gate." He was like a local judge who knew what was right but did not have the courage to enforce it. Therefore, he lived with constant, nagging, value conflict. There is no greater torment than a double-minded values system.

Please remember that these reflections on the conflict of values that Lot experienced relate to Lot's inner conflict with the truth he had received about God from Abraham. Lot was not asking God for additional information in order to make decisions. He was dealing with his problems in light of the values deposit that he possessed at the time. Unfortunately, Lot never found the moral courage to conform his decisions to what he knew was right.

Conclusion

This chapter presents a framework for processing life's decisions. This framework reflects the expectation of Romans 12:1–2. We are responsible to discern God's will on the basis of a transformed mind—one that has developed a renewed worldview and values set from biblical teaching.

It is difficult to place the content of this chapter before our biblical text analysis, because the ideas and themes presented here are derived from the study we are about to pursue! I believe, however, that this brief "big picture" presentation will help you see how the whole Bible provides a mental framework for discernment.

This chapter concludes part 1 of our journey to understand the foundations for knowing God's will. We have observed the problem of knowing, God's solution to that problem, and God's expectations expressed through Paul that we renew our minds by acquiring a biblical viewpoint. The acquisition of a biblical worldview and values set transforms the way we think and make decisions in the face of life's challenges.

Part 2

Biblical Patterns for Knowing God's Will

Thus far we have explored why we have a problem knowing God's will and how we can make decisions that are in keeping with God's revealed will. It is now time to study biblical passages that address the subject of God's will. We will systematically work our way through the Old and New Testaments in chapters 4 and 5 to see how the Bible presents the idea of knowing God's will. Then in chapter 6 we will focus on some classic passages that have traditionally been used to build models about knowing God's will and suggest how they apply to your life. Chapter 7 will argue that godly discernment from a biblical values base constitutes doing God's will.

Another goal of this section is to help you learn to read the Bible in context. Christians commonly claim to read

Scripture in context; however, achieving such a reading is a major problem in popular Christian discourse. Learning to read the Bible is the first step to knowing how to use it as a source for building a Christian worldview and values set. We need to come to grips with when the Bible is telling us what to do and when it is merely telling a story about what someone else did. Discerning when and how the Bible applies to us is to determine its "normative" nature. That is, the Bible both prescribes and describes, and you must decide which it is doing in any given passage.

An analysis of the will of God in the Old and New Testaments leads us to consider the difference between knowing God's revealed will and seeking godly discernment from that revealed will. I will propose to you that God has already revealed his will and that it is now your responsibility to work out from that revelation to practice godly discernment in your everyday decisions.

4

The Will of God
in the Old Testament

■ How did Old Testament believers order their daily decisions to live for God? How did they know if they were pleasing him? A reading of the Old Testament answers these
questions from the perspective of the believers' relationship
to the law of God. They viewed God's law as God's will. The
law reflected a relational base between God and his children. Old Testament believers ordered their lives in view
of what God had revealed about himself and his desires for
human behavior. Sometimes we reflect about how much
more complicated life is today than it used to be. We might
site the advances in medical science and the more difficult
choices we face in light of advanced technology. While
our lives may seem more complex, believers of all ages
practice the same method of decision making—validating
life's challenges by means of a biblical worldview and the

values system that proceeds from it. The illustrations may vary, but the process is the same.

Knowing God's Will the Old Testament Way

The Old Testament reveals three patterns of knowing God and his will. First, God overcame the problem of knowing by giving direct revelation about himself and his will to select persons in redemptive history. For example, God communicated his will through Abraham, Moses, and the prophets. Second, the continued presence of initial direct revelation in oral and/or written form becomes the pool, the "values deposit," providing normative guidance for God's people. The psalmists often reflect this use of Scripture. Third, several special features, such as casting of lots and the Urim and Thummim, were used on special occasions to discern the divine will.

Directly Revealed Truth

From the Garden of Eden until Moses and subsequent persons provided the written Scripture, the presence of divine truth on earth depended on God's direct revelation of himself and his will to select individuals. We rely upon Moses' account of these events, accounts he composed through every means available to him as well as any direct information God might have given him. Genesis reflects how God communicated to and through Adam and Eve, Abel and Cain, Enoch and Noah, Abram and his progeny. In addition to these major characters in biblical history, there are implications of God's broader activity with persons such as Melchizedek (Gen. 14:17–24) and Balaam (Numbers 22–24). We know virtually nothing about God's self-revealing activity outside the primary group of persons upon whom the Bible focuses.

We do know, however, that Moses is the key person God chose to provide the biblical record of himself and his will. The five books Moses composed, called the Pentateuch, provide the foundation upon which redemptive history and truth are built. Moses was a direct recipient of God's revelation (e.g., Exodus 20–34) and was called by God to reiterate the meaning of that truth in an inspired manner (cf. how Deuteronomy expands basic ideas). Even within the Pentateuch we see Moses move from receiving direct revelation to taking that database and reproclaiming it in a value-laden way. One classic example of this is the origin of the "greatest commandment" that Jesus brought into focus (Matt. 22:36–39; Luke 10:27; Lev. 19:18; Deut. 6:5; 10:12; Josh. 22:5). The great commandment was not part of God's direct revelation to Moses, but it was a summary statement developed by Moses in his repreaching of the significance of God's law.

Love captures the essential value of the relationship between God and the world at all levels. It captures God's agenda toward his creation (John 3:16); it reflects the creation's responsibility toward God (Deut. 6:5); and it controls the reciprocal relationship of those who follow God (Galatians 5–6). Love depicts the supreme value toward which we strive. It is a foundational term depicting covenant and personal relationships. Neither the law nor the whole Bible could address every situation in life that might arise. Therefore, God's followers need a model to guide their relationships. Love is that model. Love, however, is not self-defining. We must utilize God's teaching to guide love. We must also reason from God's teaching to understand what the loving thing to do is in situations not specifically addressed. This major biblical term leads us into a value discernment process.

The Revealed "Values Deposit"

Although a process of direct revelation continued through-out Old Testament history, the Bible indicates that this direct revelation was a special process for the nation of Israel and that this was not the way God expected individual believers to normally process decisions. Moses and his protégés prepared their generation to operate from the truth conveyed through these special representatives of God. Deuteronomy explicitly commands that generation to run their lives from the truth that had been revealed (6:1–9; 8:3; cf. Josh. 1:6–8). Deuteronomy 6:1–9 sets such a pattern that it requires our reading here.

> These are the commands, decrees and laws the LORD your God directed me to teach you to observe in the land that you are crossing the Jordan to possess, so that you, your children and their children after them may fear the LORD your God as long as you live by keeping all his decrees and commands that I give you, and so that you may enjoy long life. Hear, O Israel, and be careful to obey so that it may go well with you and that you may increase greatly. . . .
>
> Hear, O Israel: The LORD our God, the LORD is one. Love the LORD your God with all your heart and with all your soul and with all your strength. These commandments that I give you today are to be upon your hearts. Impress them on your children. Talk about them when you sit at home and when you walk along the road, when you lie down and when you get up. Tie them as symbols on your hands and bind them on your foreheads. Write them on the doorframes of your houses and on your gates.

The primacy of the truth deposit that Moses conveyed to the nation is crystal clear. Israel was taught to depend upon the divinely given writings of Moses as they launched into the next phase of redemptive history. This model of dependence upon already revealed truth is reflected in how the rest of the Old Testament writers refer to what has already been taught as they face their own challenges. The psalmists reflect on the law in their personal struggles, and the prophets call forth the law as a standard for the nation's responsibilities.

The historical books of the Old Testament (Joshua to Esther) chronicle Israel's life in relation to God from the perspective of covenant and law. Special individuals—Joshua, Samuel, and the early prophets like Elijah—emerge as vehicles through which God communicates to the nation. Israel as a nation, which of course is made up of individual decision makers, is viewed from the perspective of how the people relate to what Moses already taught. Life was to be lived on the basis of the truth and values of the Pentateuch.

The wisdom literature of the Old Testament particularly portrays the believer discerning life on the basis of reflection upon God's revealed Word. Job maintained his view of self in spite of circumstances and a silent heaven. He was only vindicated in hindsight (Job 42:2). The various psalmists model a reflection upon life from a biblical perspective. A well-known passage in Psalm 119 illustrates this mindset.

> How can a young man keep his way pure?
>   By living according to your word.
> I seek you with all my heart;
>   do not let me stray from your commands.
> I have hidden your word in my heart
>   that I might not sin against you.
>
> verses 9–11

Psalm 119 is famous for its constant and multifaceted way of referring to God's law. The law permeated the psalmists' reflective discernment.

The wisdom of the Proverbs also reflects how already revealed truth becomes the values deposit upon which wisdom is constructed. Proverbs 1 models wisdom as the product of knowledge that is passed on from one generation to the next. The wisdom of a parent or teacher often becomes personified into the voice of God. This voice comes from reading and listening to instruction, not seeking to hear a voice in addition to what is already available. Outside the Book of Proverbs, a fool is one who does not know God (Ps. 14:1; Jer. 4:22), but in Proverbs, "the fool" and "folly" are used as the opposite of the "wise." The wise are those who hear and obey God's instructions. The fool, however, is the antithesis of one who runs his or her life by God's teaching (Prov. 10:8, 14; 11:29; 12:15; 14:3; 17:28; 29:9). The fool in Proverbs has plenty of opportunity to be wise, but he refuses to follow the revealed truth available to him. Consequently, the product of a fool's ways is folly, the opposite of godly knowledge (Prov. 12:23; 13:16; 14:18; 15:2, 14), wisdom (14:1, 8), understanding (15:21), and prudence (16:22).[1] The whole system of knowing God and doing God's will in the Old Testament depended upon one's knowledge of the established divine teaching and how that applied to the questions of life.

The prophetic literature of the Old Testament reflects the same patterns. The writing prophets were primarily "covenant policemen." They critiqued Israel's life according to the standards of God's Word, especially the Pentateuch, and found them wanting. Although the prophets were sometimes conveyers of new truth, they were often the vehicles of God to point out how the nation had failed to fulfill the truth and values already revealed. This is at the core of understanding the values deposit as the normal procedure of discernment.

Special Provisions for Divining God's Will in the Old Testament

In addition to the dominant patterns of direct revelation to special individuals and then others living from that values deposit, the Old Testament records several special provisions. Because these procedures reflect some aspects of divination in the ancient Near Eastern historical context of Israel, we will need to survey how the world outside the Bible sought to know divine will.

Divination was a common part of the ancient Near Eastern culture. Pagan divination practices, including astrology, are condemned by God for use by Israel (Lev. 19:26; Deut. 18:9–13; 2 Kings 17:16–20). However, pagan divination practices as part of the world in which Israel functioned are reflected throughout the Old Testament. Such practices included the casting of lots (Jonah 1:7); the reading of organs, especially the liver (hepatoscopy); arrow casting (rhabdomancy, Ezek. 21:21), reading of water in vessels (hydromancy, Gen. 44:5); astrology (2 Kings 17:16; 23:4–5; Jer. 10:2–3); and mediums and spiritists (Lev. 19: 31; 1 Samuel 28; 2 Kings 17:17; Isa. 8:19–20).[2]

Isaiah makes a fascinating remark in light of our present discussion:

> When men tell you to consult mediums and spiritists, who whisper and mutter, should not a people inquire of their God? Why consult the dead on behalf of the living? To the law and to the testimony! If they do not speak according to this word, they have no light of dawn.
>
> Isaiah 8:19–20

Isaiah makes it clear that the written record of God's will is the normative way to seek knowledge about God. No matter how impressive other procedures might have seemed to Israel, they needed to know the Scripture. This sounds like Jesus' parable about the rich man and Lazarus (Luke 16). He states that the written record of Moses and the prophets has more value than a messenger returning from the dead (16:31). Like Israel of old, modern Christians waste a lot of time seeking sensational solutions to their quest to know God and his will, solutions that sometimes border on pagan divination, rather than settling down with the Good Book for a nice long read.

Even though pagan divination practices were disallowed, God gave Israel several special provisions. These provisions were not designed to satisfy the desires for "guidance-on-demand" by individual Israelites but were prominent in the guidance of major events in redemptive history.

The early, nonwriting prophets were a special provision of God for the guidance of the nation. Persons like Deborah, Gideon, Samuel, Elijah, and Elisha were direct conduits of God's will to the people. When these persons spoke on God's behalf, their words were still to be evaluated in terms of God's previously revealed truth (Deut. 13:1–5). Once God's Word was in place, oral speech that claimed to speak for God was critiqued in terms of what was already known.

Other provisions included dreams (Genesis 37; Judges 7; Daniel 7) and miraculous signs (Exodus 3; Num. 22: 28–30; Judg. 6:15–22, 36–40; 1 Sam. 14:8). These events are particularly related to key events within the development of God's redemptive plan and are not privatized situations.

God sanctioned for Israel's guidance the use of lot casting and the unique Urim and Thummim. The use of lots as a means of divination was common throughout the ancient world. There are about ninety-eight references to lots in the Old Testament. Lots were primarily used to provide a system of fairness in choice. Lots determined which animal would be sacrificed (Lev. 16:8) and were particularly prominent in decisions about land distribution (Num. 26:55; Joshua 13–21). The success of this procedure depended on a nation's worldview. Israel's worldview saw God's hand in everything. Consequently, they accepted the result of the lots process because they viewed God as sovereign. Proverbs 16:33 summarizes this: "The lot is cast into the lap, but its every decision is from the LORD." This imagery became a metaphor for life situations under the hand of God, as Jeremiah 13:25 reflects, "'This is your lot, the portion I have decreed for you,' declares the LORD." This process was also commonly accepted to settle all kinds of disputes, as Proverbs 18:18 reflects, "Casting the lot settles disputes and keeps strong opponents apart." It seems that the use of lots in Israel was more related to discernment from a worldview perspective than from a revelatory process.

The most mysterious special provision for guidance in the Old Testament is what is called the Urim and Thummim. There are less than a dozen references to these objects, in name or implied function. Their actual use seems limited to the period from the Judges to David, although they had existed since the time of Moses (Exod. 28:30). They are exclusively the property of the priest and priestly function (see Num. 27:18–21). There is no evidence that the Urim and Thummim were used after the time of David.[3] The revelatory function this priestly tool provided was probably replaced by the writing prophets.

Biblical scholars have failed to come to a consensus on the nature and usage of the Urim and Thummim. All agree that the Hebrew terms and the biblical references provide inadequate information for final definition. The two main explanations include that they are either a lot-type yes/no oracular device or that they serve a prophetic function. These items may have brought to the priesthood a revelatory and prophetic function. As the priesthood lost its touch with God and the prophets were raised up, God's use of this function seems to fall into disuse. Whatever the explanation, this unique provision no longer exists.

The Meaning of "God's Will" in the Old Testament

The phrase "will of God," as used by Christians, is more of a New Testament phrase than an Old Testament one. The direct use of this phrase is almost nonexistent in the Old Testament. The concept, however, is present in the use of other terms.

What Does It Mean to Fulfill the "Will" of Another Person?

A study of what it means to fulfill someone's will yields a broad continuum of meaning. On one end of the continuum, to do someone's will means to conform to the known expectations of a person you desire to please. Phrases like "desire to please," "to delight in," and "to find favor" dominate these kinds of contexts (Num. 11:11; Ruth 2:2; 2 Sam. 14:22). In the Old Testament, the psalmist uses the phrasing, "I rejoice in following your statutes" (119:14), whereas the New Testament would say, "My food is to do the will of him who sent me" (John 4:34). This end of the continuum provides one with an opportunity to please another. It is a matter of choice from our own internal motivation. On the other end of the continuum, to do someone's will means to fulfill the irresistible purpose of a person of power. To do the will of a king is not a choice, but a command performance.

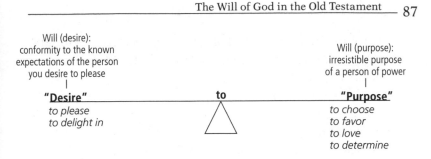

Fig. 8. Continuum for Term *Will*

The continuum of "desire to purpose" also represents the relationship of humankind to God in the Old Testament. Solomon reflects on this continuum in Proverbs 21:1–3 when he sees an earthly king subject to God's will on one hand and God desiring a right heart over externalism on the other hand. Those who follow God desire to do his will. The psalmist reflects on the delight of doing God's will (40:8) as well as the desire for God to help one be obedient to his will (143:10). God is also viewed as one who can enforce his purposes upon the earth, as Job (42:3 ASV) and even a pagan king testify. Daniel reports Nebuchadnezzar's insight into God's will,

> And all the inhabitants of the earth are accounted as
>   nothing,
> But He does according to His will in the host of heaven
> And among the inhabitants of earth;
> And no one can ward off His hand
> Or say to Him, "What hast Thou done?"
>
> Daniel 4:35 NASB

What Does It Mean to Fulfill God's Will in the Old Testament?

The Old Testament presents God's will in two ways: God's sovereign purposes and God's moral instruction. There are certain purposes of God that he will bring to pass regardless of human involvement or cooperation. Job's journey was not an easy one. In fact, some might even say, "Wow, would God really allow that to happen to one of his children?" In the end, Job recognized God's sovereignty and stated, "I know that thou canst do all things, And that no purpose of thine can be restrained" (42:2 ASV). The psalmist reflects that the angelic realm fulfills the sovereign purposes of God (103:20–22). Even the mind and will of earthly kings are sometimes subject to God's control (Prov. 21:1). Isaiah particularly outlines God's sovereign will over the nations of the earth (25:1; 44:28; 46:10; 48:14; cf. Ezra 5:17 with 7:18). God's sovereignty—his providential behind-the-scenes control—is a major part of the fabric of the Joseph narrative in Genesis, the Book of Esther, and the historical material in Daniel.

In addition to God's sovereign control, he has placed information about his desires before us so that we might respond. God's requirements are primarily stated in his moral instructions. God's revealed truth constitutes *the* major way we know and do God's will in the Bible. Ezra dealt with the intermarriage crises (Ezra 9–10) as a breach of God's moral will for Israel (cf. 10:11). The psalmist particularly reflects on how God's moral instructions provide guidance for life. Psalm 23:1–3 views God's revealed righteousness as a guide for life. God's will and God's law are equated in the mind of the Old Testament believer (Ps. 40:8). When the psalmist prays, "Teach me to do your will, for you are my God" (143:10), the focus is on bringing oneself into submission to what God has already taught rather than praying for new information.

The prophet Daniel had a long and significant career. Nebuchadnezzar took him captive, and he entered exile in Babylon in 605 B.C.E. He maintained his Jewish identity in the face of many obstacles and arose to prominent positions within his host country. Daniel was used of God in special ways to convey prophetic truth to his generation for nearly seventy years (605–536 B.C.E.). Daniel was a special recipient of direct revelation from God. He recognized that without God's intervention, we would be left to our own inadequate devices (Dan. 2:20–23).

At the same time, Daniel provides an interesting illustration of how an Old Testament believer ordered his life around God's moral will. Daniel lived his daily life on the basis of previously revealed truth. Daniel 1, where the newly captive Daniel and a few friends refused to participate in the prescribed food and drink menu of the Babylonians, is a well-known story of courage. But why did they refuse this menu? Some would say because it violated the food laws of the Pentateuch. But wine was never forbidden in the food laws. The more probable reason that Daniel and his friends refused these items is that they were tainted by participation in the pagan temple rites. Daniel would not defile himself by participation with food blessed through a pagan system (cf. Exod. 34:15; 1 Corinthians 8–10; Isa. 52:11). He chose to maintain ritual purity according to the law. At a later time, Daniel would not even deviate from holy customs he had adopted in his worship of God. He continued his habit of prayer in spite of the possible consequences (Daniel 6). The nature of Daniel's prayer life had customary background in Jewish life (see 1 Kings 8:35; Ps. 55:17; 1 Esd. 4:58), but it was not a matter of law.

Conclusion

The Old Testament records the history of God revealing himself to the world and the choice of Abraham's seed as the nation in which he would focus this revelation.

As the deposit of God's teaching grew, the people of God reflected a dependence upon that body of teaching to order their lives. Moses established the pattern in Deuteronomy, and the Psalms and Prophets reflect the same pattern hundreds of years later. Doing God's will meant obeying God's commands.

Chapter 6 will treat several special examples of Old and New Testament passages and events that are often used in promoting models of God's will. We must first, however, delineate the New Testament's statements about knowing the will of God.

5

The Will of God
in the New Testament

■ The question "What is God's will for my life?" is a distinct part of American evangelical Christian culture. Our focus in the question is often on "my life." This reflects the "me" generation of Western culture. It grows out of the intense demand for a "privatized" religious experience resulting from Western Christianity drinking too deeply from the wells of its own culture. An almost unconscious assumption exists among Christians today that their personal lives are at the center of what is important in the universe. "Mall churches" spring up to meet our every demand. Excessive attention to the Christian consumer mentality has become a central value in many ministries.

This individualized mindset has influenced how some understand the biblical idea of "God's will." God certainly does have a will for my life, but the Bible, not culture, must define what this means. God's commands, and the derived values they provide, constitute a personalized will for every creature under heaven. Many believers miss God's will because they are looking in the wrong place.

The privatized emphasis of our culture is not the mindset of either an Old Testament or a New Testament believer. The believers' struggle over God's will in the biblical record centers on the effort to "do" God's will. They do not model a process of "finding" God's will, because they had already received it. They understood God's will to be equivalent with the truth and behavior patterns he had revealed as his desires for his people. They were more concerned with growing in their understanding of God's revelation and living up to the standards they knew pleased God rather than with gaining additional information about the future.

Understanding the "Will of God" in the New Testament

The New Testament provides a focused linguistic database to study what God's will means. Forty-nine texts in the New Testament contain the noun *will* with a divine designation (e.g., "will of God," "will of the Lord," "your will," etc.). Paul's writings provide twenty examples and the rest are spread out in the Books of Matthew (five), Mark (one), Luke (two), John (seven), Acts (two), Hebrews (five), Peter (four), 1 John (two), and Revelation (one).

We can group these examples into a number of categories to describe their usage. Such an analysis is a first step in organizing the data. I've kept the list simple to illustrate the process of doing a word study in the Bible.

> 1. Conformity to do the will of God is an evidence of being a member of God's family (Matt. 7:21; 12:50; Mark 3:35).

2. God's will is his declared program (related to sovereignty, overlaps with category 3. Matt. 26:42; John 6: 38–40; Acts 13:36; Rom. 9:19; Gal. 1:4; Eph. 1:5, 9–10).

3. The will of God recognizes God's control of circumstances (Acts 21:14; Rom. 1:10; 15:32; 1 Peter 3:17; 4:19).

4. The prominent phrase, "through the will of God," stands for the idea of "according to God's sovereign plan" (1 Cor. 1:1; 2 Cor. 1:1; 8:5; Eph. 1:1; Col. 1:1; 2 Tim. 1:1; Rev. 4:11).

5. The verb *to do* dominates will of God references. The contexts indicate that *to do* means to conform one's attitude and behavior to what is already known (cf. category 1. Matt. 21:31; Luke 12:47; John 4:34; 5:30; 6:38; 7:17; 9:31; Acts 13:22; Eph. 6:6; Heb. 10:7, 9, 36; 13:21; 1 John 2:17).

6. The will of God is declared or already known, including exhortations to know or understand, and therefore merely requires our obedience (Matt. 18:14; Rom. 12:2; Eph. 5:17; Col. 1:9; 4:12; 1 Thess. 4:3; 5:18; 1 Peter 2:15).

7. God's will is in contrast to man's will (1 Peter 4:2).

8. God's [sovereign?] will as a standard for prayer (Matt. 6:10; Luke 11:2; 22:42; 1 John 5:14).

This information yields several major assertions about God's will in the New Testament.

The Phrase "Will of God" Is Used to Refer to God's Sovereign Will

The sovereignty of God is an idea derived from biblical teaching that God is the supreme being of the universe. God is in a different class than his creation. God is the supreme and independent director and authority for all created reality. How God's sovereignty is applied to his creation is a matter for the Bible itself to define.[1]

As in the Old Testament, God's sovereignty accounts for a significant portion of how the New Testament images the will of God. Jesus' coming to earth to fulfill the redemptive plan was part of God's sovereign will (John 6:38–40). The death of Christ as necessary to fulfill the plan of salvation was clear in Jesus' mind (Matt. 26:42). The apostles viewed salvation by the redemptive work of Christ to be an aspect of God's sovereign will (Gal. 1:4; Eph. 1:3–10). God's sovereign prerogatives were foundational to Paul's understanding of God's saving grace to the Gentiles (Rom. 9:19 in its context).

The Bible calls for us to have a God-centered world-view. This is reflected in statements about God's control of the circumstances of life. James 4:15 exhorted an early group of believers who assumed that they directed the circumstances of their own lives to pause and realize that ultimately "If it is the Lord's will, we will live and do this or that." Paul deeply desired to go to Rome. He, however, recognized that such a visit had to fall within God's control of his life circumstances (Rom. 1:10; 15:32).

Paul's journey to Jerusalem presents a most interesting case of God's sovereign will in relation to Paul's life circumstances (Acts 20–21). Paul had decided that he needed to be in Jerusalem by the day of Pentecost (20:16). This had become a settled conviction for him, a conviction that he attributed to the Spirit (20:22), without framing it in a revelatory context. His burden became known and he himself believed that this trip would bring an end to his freedom (20:22–24). As he passed through areas and visited with converts, they, "through the Spirit" (21:4), argued with Paul about his decision to go to Jerusalem. Agabus, a recognized prophet, prophesied in a graphic manner Paul's imprisonment (21:10–11). On the basis of this divine revelation about Paul's life circumstances, the believers argued even more with Paul about his plans. While Acts is abbreviated in its content, they must have discussed these issues with Paul at great length and with much passion. Paul, however, remained firm in his decision in spite of the exceedingly rare advantage of knowing God's sovereign will in advance (21:12–17). Paul's friends finally resigned themselves not to interfere with God's sovereign will (21:14).

Paul's self-understanding was conditioned by submission to God's divine plan. He had earlier preached about King David's life as an example of God's overall control of one's world (Acts 13:36). The King James Version translates this text as "by the will of God," and the New International Version translates it as "God's purpose." The Greek word here may be translated either way, but it is a more focused term denoting God's direct determination and therefore the New International Version chooses the term *purpose* (cf. Acts 2:23). The perspective that our life circumstances, even down to our vocations, are a part of God's determinate will is also reflected in the often-repeated phrase "through the will of God." This phrase is particularly used by Paul to justify God's appointment of him as an apostle (1 Cor. 1:1; 2 Cor. 1:1; 8:5; Eph. 1:1; Col. 1:1; 2 Tim. 1:1; cf. Rev. 4:11).

Peter wrote to a community that was undergoing severe trials. They faced life-threatening situations and the threat of physical harm. Peter appeals to God's sovereign will as a way to bring divine reason to human suffering (1 Peter 4:19). Peter used Christ as an example of one who did good and yet suffered for it within God's will (1 Peter 3:17). Knowing that doing good was not a ticket to bypass suffering brought some comfort to Peter's audience. The early Christians were able to accept that although God was able to intervene on their behalf, it was all right if he chose not to do so. God's choice was part of his sovereign discretion and not contradictory to his goodness.

Viewing God as sovereign over the circumstances of life is an important aspect of a biblical worldview. God's presence in this sense does not alleviate human responsibility. Our responsibility is addressed by other categories of God's will.

The Phrase "Will of God" Represents God's Moral Teaching

In the Old Testament, God's will was equivalent to his law in the understanding of the Old Testament believer. If we asked Old Testament believers, "Do you know God's will for your life?" they would look at us a bit oddly and say, "But of course!" Then they would tell us that God's will for their life is to love God and love their neighbor as they obey his commands. The New Testament pattern is the same. The phrases and sentences that portray this subject may differ slightly between the testaments due to time and culture, but the ideas are the same.

In the New Testament, God's will is often equivalent with his teaching. Paul reflects the connection with the Old Testament in Romans 2:17–18 where he concludes that God's will and the law are equivalent. Paul set a high value on God's Word, viewing the possession of the revealed Word as the highest privilege of a Jew (Rom. 3:1–2). Other examples of equating God's will with biblical teaching include texts where the statement "this *is* God's will" is followed by moral teaching. This is observed in 1 Thessalonians 4:3–8: "It is God's will that you should be sanctified: that you should [fulfill these moral instructions]." First Thessalonians 5:18

concludes a series of exhortations with "This is God's will for you in Christ Jesus." 1 Peter 2:15, in the midst of a moral exhortation context, states, "For it is God's will that by doing good you should silence the ignorant talk of foolish men." In these kinds of contexts the content of God's will is the teaching in the texts themselves.

The Gospels contain a statement that has often troubled the casual reader. Matthew 7:21 states, "Not everyone who says to me, 'Lord, Lord,' will enter the kingdom of heaven, but only *he who does the will of my Father* who is in heaven" (emphasis added) (cf. Matt. 12:50; Mark 3:35). Some have struggled to explain that this phrase does not contradict Ephesians 2:8–9, where Paul denies works as a means to grace but views them as a product of grace (Eph. 2:10). There is no conflict between Jesus and Paul; they are looking at two sides of a coin. Jesus in the Gospels states that conformity to God's revealed will, namely his moral teachings, is an evidence of true salvation. False professors who speak the name of the Lord but do not show the evidence of salvation in their lives will not fool God and will not enter heaven. Jesus and the Gospel writers portray salvation very much like the Old Testament. They view righteousness as an act of obedience to God's teaching. Paul tends to image salvation from the legal viewpoint, indicating who we are in our standing before God. The Gospel statements about "he who does the will of my Father" tie God's will to God's commands. They are equivalent.

The fact that God's will constitutes his teaching accounts for the presence of the verb *do* as the dominant verb in "will of God" passages. Contrary to the common stereotype about God's will, the Bible never exhorts a believer to "find" God's will. There is no need to find it because it has never been lost. Perhaps the reason we often feel like we cannot "find" an answer to our questions is because we are demanding that the Bible yield information it was not designed to yield. If we process our questions appropriately, they will answer themselves, because answers flow from a well-understood biblical worldview. We are constantly exhorted to "do" God's will, assuming a pool of knowledge to which the believer can respond. Doing God's will is not a search for unrevealed information in order to make a decision. Rather, we are to conform our attitudes and behavior to what God has already taught in his Word. This is part of the fabric of the teaching of Jesus (Matt. 21: 31; Luke 12:47; John 4:34; 5:30; 6:38; 7:17; 9:31) and of the apostles (Eph. 6:6; Heb. 10:7, 9, 36; 13:21; 1 John 2:17).

A surface reading of "will of God" passages where verbs like *know, be filled with,* or *understand* are used have caused some to think that these terms are synonyms for *find.* Such an understanding, however, is not true to the biblical contexts. These exhortations are not invitations to obtain new revelation but are appeals to engage the information already available. The contexts of these kinds of phrases are usually self-defining and focused on the believer's growth in obedience to God's revealed truth.

How New Testament Passages Exhort the Acquisition of God's Will

New Testament exhortations to "know," "be filled with," or "understand" God's will need special attention. Such passages require that the reader understand Paul's religious language in the context of an epistle, a letter from one party to another. Think of an epistle as a one-way telephone conversation. Paul is calling his friends, with whom he has already shared a lot of information, and reminding them about his former instruction. When Paul makes an abbreviated statement in a letter, the recipients know the assumed information that Paul only needs to suggest. They understand each other, but we only have Paul's end of the telephone. Therefore, we must be conscious of the assumed pool of knowledge existing between these two parties. Let us review some key passages with these issues in view. Colossians provides us a good example.

> For this reason, since the day we heard about you, we have not stopped praying for you and asking God to fill you with the knowledge of his will through all spiritual wisdom and understanding. And we pray this in order that you may live a life worthy of the Lord and may please him in every way: bearing fruit in every good work, growing in the knowledge of God, being strengthened with all power according to his glorious might so that you may have great endurance and patience, and joyfully giving thanks to the Father, who has qualified you to share in the inheritance of the saints in the kingdom of light.
>
> Colossians 1:9–12

Paul's prayer is that the Colossians be "filled" with the knowledge of God's will. The term *fill* is a metaphor that needs explanation. The literal meaning of *fill*, "to increase the content of a container," is not to be imported into Paul's statement. Paul's religious language especially makes use of this metaphor. He speaks of being filled with unrighteousness (Rom. 1:29), knowledge (Rom. 15:14), comfort (2 Cor. 7:4), the Spirit (Eph. 5:18), the fruits of righteousness (Phil. 1:11), and joy (2 Tim. 1:4). These contexts are about what characterizes our lives. *Characterize* bests explains the metaphorical use of *fill* in Colossians 1:9. Paul desired that these believers' lives be characterized by the spiritual truth that they already knew. Paul made it clear in Colossians 1: 3–8 that the Colossian believers were taught God's truth by Paul's protégé, Epaphras (1:5–7), and that they had exempli-

fied that truth to all the saints (1:4). He now prays for the
Colossians to continue and increase in what was already a
reality. The application of God's Word fulfills Paul's exhortation to "live a life worthy of the Lord and . . . please him in
every way: bearing fruit in every good work, growing in the
knowledge of God" (1:10).

Paul's use of *fill* as a metaphor of characterization is
also illustrated in Ephesians 5:17–18: "Understand what
the Lord's will is . . . be filled with the Spirit." In this case,
"understand" is not a command to find something but to
consider what is about to be stated. The focus is on what
is announced as the Lord's will, namely, "be filled with
the Spirit." It is often claimed that *fill* means "control"
in Ephesians 5:18. But this imagery does not help the
reader fulfill this command. The meaning of *characterize* may be seen by comparing the use of *fill* in Acts 9:36.
Acts relates the story of Dorcas, a female disciple who
was particularly known for her good works. The literal
translation of verse 36 is that "this woman was full of
good works" (notice the interpretive translation of the
NIV, "was always doing good"). We would not want to say
that Dorcas was *controlled* by good works! Rather, she was
characterized by this godly lifestyle. To be filled with the
Spirit is best understood as being characterized by the
kind of life that the Spirit promotes, a life lived according
to the behavioral patterns promoted in the moral teaching of the Bible.

Many Christians have an "Almond Joy" idea about
being filled with the Spirit. It is an "indescribably deli-
cious" experience that we all desire but do not know how
to realize. This ambiguity was not Paul's intent. He used
this metaphor to encourage his readers to show forth, to
be characterized by biblical teaching so that we can reflect
the image of God here on earth. Compare Ephesians 5:18

to Colossians 3:16, where being filled with the Spirit is replaced by "Let the word of Christ dwell in you richly."

Paul's reference to being filled "with the knowledge of his will" (Col. 1:9) reminds a reader of Romans 2:18, where Paul reflects that the Jews knew "his will." These kinds of expressions portray information that the audience possesses, not something that they have to find. Colossians 4:12 also reminds us of the Old Testament use of *will* as the equivalent of God's Word. Epaphras prays that they "may stand firm in all the will of God, mature and fully assured." Epaphras's desire was that these believers grow in their convictions about what they already knew. They did not need more information in order to know or do God's will. They merely needed to maintain and strengthen their internal conviction to live as they had been taught (refer back to Col. 1:6–7).

We can strengthen our understanding of Paul's religious language in Colossians 1:9 by comparing Philippians 1: 9–11, where Paul says the same thing in different words without the "will of God" formula.

> And this is my prayer: that your love may abound more and more in knowledge and depth of insight, so that you may be able to discern what is best and may be pure and blameless until the day of Christ, filled with the fruit of righteousness that comes through Jesus Christ—to the glory of and praise of God.

Here, Paul uses the language of being "filled with the fruit of righteousness" rather than being filled with the knowledge of God's will. Did Paul think of these variant ways of phrasing as conveying two completely different ideas? I don't think so. If we could sit down and discuss this with Paul, he would say that he meant the same thing in both places. He was burdened that both sets of believers progress in applying God's truth to life. This was truth that was already revealed and they knew it. He now urges them to increase the way their lives characterize the moral teaching of God. Abounding in knowledge and insight (Phil. 1:9) is the product of pursuing the transformed mind of Romans 12:1–2. Discerning what decisions to make in life is not a magical process but the consistent acquisition, processing, and application of God's Word (Phil. 1:10).

A closer look at the passages just reviewed illustrates that references to God's will are in contexts where believers are being exhorted to live up to what they know. They have been taught adequate information about what God requires and merely need to increase their commitment to do God's will. Discernment, therefore, is about the application of truth. The New Testament never explains decision-making discernment as some kind of search for new information. God's will is not something we need to find; it is discovered in the application of revealed truth to daily living. This is true for the individual believer and for the church as a corporate community. Decisions we observe in the Book of Acts are derived from the church's discussion and community consensus under the Spirit's conviction.

Conclusion

New Testament texts that directly address the subject of God's will reflect the same patterns as the Old Testament. God has a sovereign and a moral will. His *sovereign* will is reflected in the provision of a redemptive plan and the general supervision of life circumstances. The early Christians did not seek to know the content of God's sovereign actions, they merely submitted to certain circumstances in life as part of God's overall control. They exercised their responsibility to the best of their ability and then rested in the results as part of God's plan.

God's *moral* will is presented in biblical teaching about attitudes and behavior. Commands and exhortations about living are given, and believers are then responsible to transform their lives into conformity with God's teaching. Alignment with this teaching becomes the criteria to judge one's salvation and spirituality. The New Testament does not present a model of searching for God's will in order to make decisions. Rather, the pattern is to respond to biblical teaching and use that teaching to order our lives.

This, however, is not all there is to discerning God's will for our lives. Many of the decisions with which we struggle do not fall conveniently within the direct statements of Scripture. Decisions about what house, car, or computer to buy and when to spend the money do not require a biblical proof text, although our values will affect these decisions. Neither does the Bible suggest that we appeal to God to reveal his sovereign will or to give us omniscient insight into the future. We must process life issues from a biblical worldview and values system. From biblical teaching we learn to derive sound reasons for decisions that cannot be addressed with a simple proof text. This process is part of God's plan to develop us after his image.

6

Is Every Example
in the Bible for Me?

■ As a pastor and professor, I have had a number of interesting experiences with people and their perceptions of God's will for their lives. Far too many of these experiences relate to misunderstandings about God's will. I was once drawn into a counseling situation with a young man who was fixated on a certain young woman. He was convinced that God had called her to marry him. He conveyed to me numerous reasons why he knew this to be true. His reasons related to applying certain examples from the Old Testament where God dealt with a certain person in a certain way. He claimed that God had given him a number of signs that identified this woman as the one. Unfortunately, she did not get the same message! This was humorous at first. The humor soon faded as this young man began to stalk the young lady in an effort to bring her into conformity with his view of God's will. Eventually the police had to intervene. Even after this measure, I continued to receive occasional calls at odd times of the night from this poor fellow about his need to enforce God's will.

On another occasion, at a seminar on God's will, a young woman testified about why she had never had a car wreck on her way to school and work. She claimed the phrase, "I being in the way, the LORD led me" (Gen. 24:27 KJV). She told about how she was sensitive to impressions about which way to turn at each stop sign. The fact that she had never had a wreck was proof to her of God's guidance. I think her daily trips were at least scenic.

These may seem extreme examples, but I think too many Christians can identify with the methods behind them. We need now to review some of the examples in the Old and New Testaments that are often used to claim patterns for seeking God's will.

Some have developed models of knowing God's will by taking biblical accounts of how God has dealt with persons and events recorded in the Bible and asserted that this is the way we should do it today. Gideon "putting out the fleece" is adapted into modern terms to "test the waters" for God's will. We are told we should request from God some sort of "sign" to give him the opportunity to "show" us the way. We assume that if God led his people in a certain manner in the past, the same procedures are still available for our use. Yet, how many believers who try to practice these kinds of processes find themselves frustrated with either a silent heaven or bad results after a decision is made? Such experiences usually require us to explain why it is not God's fault that we made a bad decision. Or we live in denial of our anger against God for letting us down.

What can we learn from biblical examples? How do we know if we should follow the same process we observe in a biblical story? First, we must learn to read the Bible in its historical context. Then we need to be aware of how to draw principles from all of Scripture without violating the teaching intent of a given passage.

Learning to Read the Bible All Over Again

When we were children, we learned a song in Sunday school:

> Every promise in the Book is mine,
>   every chapter, every verse, every line.

This song conditioned us to read the Bible as if it were a plastic "bread of life" box of promise cards from our kitchen table rather than a story of how God has dealt with various believing generations. The song is not true. The target audience of a given promise is determined by the context in which it is given. Not all promises or commands are universal. The biblical story is a progressively developing dialogue between God and his people. As circumstances change, so do the methods by which the dialogue takes place and the content for which we are responsible. The Bible is an accurate record of the dialogue. How we relate the details of this conversation between God and his people to ourselves is a challenge for biblical interpretation and theology. All Christians are responsible to use the Bible in appropriate ways. This is not a task for pastors and theologians alone.

There is a dictum among Bible interpreters. For biblical passages, "there is one interpretation but many applications." The problem is that the *m* has been removed from the word *many,* and therefore *any*thing soon becomes the meaning of a text. In order to draw guidance from the

Bible, however, we must learn to use it in an appropriate manner.

How Does the Bible Teach Us? (Direct, Implied, and Creative Constructs)

The Bible was written over a fifteen hundred–year period (about 1450 B.C.E. to C.E. 100). It was addressed to the people of God in what we now view as two distinct audiences, Israel and the church. How do Christians today draw guidance from a book written over such a long and diverse period with different recipients in the minds of the authors?

Second Timothy 3:16 states, "All Scripture is God-breathed and is useful for teaching, rebuking, correcting and training in righteousness." Such a statement calls for us to determine how to utilize the total Bible, both Old and New Testaments, in our worldview and values development. In order to do this, we need a view of how the Bible as a whole teaches us, as well as an understanding of how we construct our own views on applying its teaching in our situations.

The Bible teaches us by providing a record of how God has dealt with his people throughout redemptive history up to about C.E. 100. Its record contains historical narratives, laws and commands, inspired poetic reflections, and other literary genres. Christians view the teaching of the Bible as authoritative for life and practice, faith and duty. Christian communities all recognize a progression within Scripture that defines how the Bible's teaching is to be interpreted and applied to succeeding generations both within and beyond the period of Scripture production. Yet not all communities agree on how past teaching applies to the present community. Views range from a naive total continuity, everything applies now as it did then, to a severe restriction of gleaning applicable teaching from only a few of Paul's Epistles. As you might expect, the better approach is to be found not in the extremes of the continuum but in a reasoned understanding of the nature of the record of redemptive history.

Biblical teaching is both observed (descriptive material) and obeyed (prescriptive material) on the basis of how a faith community understands the normative nature of any given passage. A normative text is one containing a command or exhortation that transcends time and audience and universally requires the obedience of all God's people. A command such as "do not steal" is timeless. A command not to intermingle two kinds of cloth, however, is considered to be limited in its application, because it addresses certain issues within a limited time and culture. The task of biblical interpretation is to determine what is or is not a normative teaching. It is helpful when both testaments give the same command, but it is not required that the New Testament repeat normative truth of the Old Testament. The laws of incest illustrate this fact in that the New Testament does not repeat what is evident to all. There is a good deal of unity in the church about what is normative, but various traditions do debate certain details.

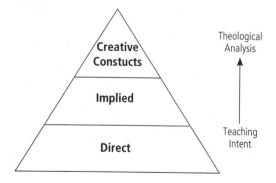

Fig. 9. Three Levels of Teaching

The Christian community develops biblical teaching at three levels: direct, implied, and creative constructs. There are passages that speak directly to an issue but have a limited shelf life, such as "Do not cook a young goat in its mother's milk" (Exod. 23:19) or "Greet one another with a holy kiss" (Rom. 16:16; 1 Cor. 16:20; 2 Cor. 13:12; 1 Thess. 5:26). There are also passages that all perceive as transcending time and culture. Examples might include terse and direct commands such as "do not lie," "do not steal," "do not commit adultery," or perhaps Paul exhorting communities to turn from idols to Jesus. Most readers sense the difference between teaching that has a normative ring to it and statements designed for a limited time period.

There is also a level of *implied* teaching, which can be called upon to represent crucial areas of theology. For instance, no text in the Bible states there is a Trinity, but Christian scholars agree that the concept of Trinity correctly represents the "plain" teaching of the Bible about the Father, Son, and Holy Spirit. When we bring modern questions to the Bible, it is often the implied teaching of Scripture to which we appeal. Issues such as abortion, euthanasia, and spousal abuse illustrate the need for this kind of interpretation from the Bible.

The third level of teaching is the development of *creative constructs*. This is the larger-picture type of teaching. Theological leaders within Christian communities look at the whole Bible and argue for a certain macro view of biblical teaching. That is, they create systems of theology that they believe account for the whole Bible. Calvinism, Arminianism, covenantalism, dispensationalism, millennialism, views of counseling, and such are creative theological constructs that various believing communities argue best represent the whole teaching of Scripture. When one decides upon a system, the tendency is to read the details of the Bible from that viewpoint.

Many Christians operate with the assumption that a surface reading of the Bible combined with "what it means to me" provides accurate information to guide our lives. Unfortunately, this simplistic approach demeans Scripture and robs the reader of its treasures. Life is not simple. Developing a biblical worldview and values set is not simple either. Understanding the broad concepts of the nature of the Bible's teaching and how we construct that teaching into a model advances our ability to use Christian discernment.

For Me or Not for Me, That Is the Question (The Issues of Prescription and Description)

Using the Bible as a guide for discernment requires that we gain skill in understanding what the Bible *prescribes* and what it *describes*. That is, we need to understand if a command, promise, or example is currently in force (prescription) or whether the text is simply a record of how God dealt with someone in the past (description). A text could be prescriptive during one period and descriptive during another (e.g., the food laws and other social stipulations). The Ten Commandments of Exodus 20, for example, are certainly prescriptive in the Old Testament. Except for how to understand the command about the Sabbath, the Ten Commandments continue to be normative (prescriptive). One test for whether an Old Testament command continues is to see if the New Testament makes similar statements, as it does with nine of the Ten Commandments. This test may be too simple, however, since we view many issues prescribed in the Old Testament as still binding even when the New Testament does not repeat the stipulation (e.g., issues of incest). Some commands are obviously normative to us because of our understanding of the nature of God and how the whole Bible represents certain issues. Nonnormative passages can also provide principles for how we deal with life today (e.g., rules about how to treat neighbors, employees, etc.). Bible scholars provide considerable discussion on how to make judgments as we deal with the Bible and ethical obligations.[1]

Another common example to consider is the Old Testament food laws. God gave Israel an elaborate set of food laws as part of the code of holiness (see Leviticus 11; Deuteronomy 14). In so doing, God prescribed certain dietary regulations for Israel, which became a major bone of contention during the transition from Judaism to Jesus in the New Testament period (see Acts 15; Galatians 2). To address this problem, God gave Peter a vision in Acts 10 that most agree transferred the Old Testament regulations from a prescriptive to a descriptive status. The change in applying the food laws would have happened naturally as the shift in identity from Israel to the church developed. Peter's vision merely expedited the process of transition. The food laws are no longer used as a code for holiness but are now, for the Christian, a part of describing Israel's history. Therefore, Christians do not use the food laws to prescribe dietary rules for the church, and these texts are not applied to our current decisions about eating.[2]

The question of whether a text is prescriptive or descriptive arises in conversations about whether Christians should observe Old Testament Sabbath regulations. There are broad differences of opinion about how or whether such a law transfers into Christian usage. Some groups maintain a Saturday Sabbath pattern. Others transfer certain restrictions into a Christian Sabbath pattern applied to Sunday. Others see no ongoing Sabbath pattern requirement. All views, however, deviate more or less from the original Old Testament and Jewish stipulations as they create their own understandings. Consequently, each group determines the delineation of prescriptive and descriptive texts as it justifies its position. Making decisions about this issue illustrates the necessity of theological analysis in using the Bible as a guide for life.

Discerning how the Bible applies to our lives is not a simple task. We must learn to appreciate the whole scope of the Bible within its historical and cultural development. When the Bible is merely describing events within redemptive history, we do not abandon it as irrelevant material. We must, however, have reasons for applying what we read to our current life situations. We cannot deal with the Bible like a ventriloquist deals with a dummy, manipulating it to say what we want it to say.

When the Bible Stops and We Start (Determining Teaching Intent and Theological Analysis)

Every biblical text has an immediate context and a meaning within that context. Together these determine the meaning of a passage. We need to understand, to whatever extent possible, the original meaning of a text in order to answer the question "What did the writer intend to teach in this particular text?" When we determine the answer, we have uncovered what is known as the "teaching intent" of the passage. It is what we believe the original author intended to teach. The Bible, however, is bigger in its teaching than the intent of its individual contexts. For example, the Bible does not address the issue of spousal or child abuse in modern terms. Does that mean that we cannot claim that the Bible is sufficient for all of faith and practice? No. The church must take the questions of its current culture to the text of

Scripture and do what we call theological analysis. What is true for the church as a community is also true for us as individuals. In a sense, theological analysis starts where the teaching intent of an individual passage ends. Theological analysis brings the implications of the biblical teaching to bear on current questions. For example, while we do not have a text on abuse, we certainly have teaching about the dignity and the required respect we should have for people created in the image of God. The Bible exhorts kindness not meanness, giving not selfishness. From these extended teachings God expects us to use the good sense he gave us to construct beliefs about the questions and challenges of life.

It does not take long to learn that many of the burdens of our lives are not addressed by teaching intent passages. Rather, we must address our questions and challenges by larger theological reflection. This is the essence of developing worldview and values thinking. This is what the command to be transformed by the renewing of our minds is all about.

Reading the Old Testament

Books about knowing God's will sometimes claim as prescribed patterns examples of how God has guided believers in times past. These examples are often chosen because of certain phrases in the text that can be used to promote guidance methods. Yet the details of stories of persons like Moses, Joshua, and Elijah are understood by almost everyone as descriptive of special events within redemptive history rather than prescriptive. Let's examine a few classic examples sometimes used in guidance literature to promote particular views of seeking God's will.

A Bride for Isaac

The story of Abraham's obtaining Rebekah for Isaac in Genesis 24 is often used as an example for guidance. Abraham's servant was sent on a journey to fetch Isaac a wife. In the process, he prayed that God would guide him by ordering circumstances in a certain way.

> Then he prayed, "O Lord, God of my master Abraham, give me success today, and show kindness to my master Abraham. See, I am standing beside this spring, and the daughters of the townspeople are coming out to draw water. May it be that when I say to a girl, 'Please let down your jar that I may have a drink,' and she says, 'Drink, and I'll water your camels too'—let her be the one you have chosen for your servant Isaac. By this I will know that you have shown kindness to my master."
>
> Before he had finished praying, Rebekah came out with her jar on her shoulder. She was the daughter of Bethuel son of Milcah, who was the wife of Abraham's brother Nahor.
>
> Genesis 24:12–15

Should believers today adopt the servant's method of discernment? If, for example, we have three job offers, should we pray that God will cause the right one to call us first, or perhaps second to make it more specific? Or should we select a life partner in a similar manner? If you answer yes, then you are taking this as a prescriptive passage. If no, then you understand it as descriptive and you must draw wisdom from it in a less direct manner.

A number of interesting features about Genesis 24 support Abraham as operating from a value-laden perspective based on God's direct revelation to him. His primary concern was for Isaac to maintain the family line because God's promise of a seed to Abraham (Gen. 12:1–3) depended on this feature. Abraham moved to protect this promise and sent the servant to the family home (24:4). This was not a chance journey; no other connection would do. The servant was fishing in the right pond. Furthermore, this is not just any event. This is a major event within redemptive history over which God exercises sovereign control. Abraham and the servant fulfilled God's moral command for them by going to the home clan. The servant's prayer was an aspect of submission to God's plan. The placement of Rebekah in the right place at the right time was part of God's providential control of these circumstances. This is a beautiful descriptive account of God's grace in redemptive history. It is not a passage that is intended to prescribe that future generations utilize the same methods. It does, however, teach us to maintain the values under which we are called if we are to place ourselves where God can bless us.

Gideon's Fleece

Another Old Testament story that people often imitate to determine God's will is found in Judges 6, the story of Gideon "putting out the fleece." Gideon was a warrior and a special person who loved God (v. 12). He was also hard to convince that God was really with him in the endeavors the angel of the Lord directed. Gideon began by requiring of the angel an initial sign of a sacrifice consumed by fire (vv. 20–22). He was rather taken with the stories he had heard about God's miracles in the Exodus and desired some external confirmation of God's presence (v. 13). Perhaps his first request for a sign was not so unreasonable. But demanding external signs in order to believe seemed to be a pattern with Gideon, a trait that eventually became a problem (see Judg. 8:25–27). Nevertheless, God accommodated Gideon's unbelief when Gideon repeatedly used a lamb's fleece to discern the reality of God's communications to him (6:36–40). God caused it to be wet or dry as Gideon requested. God was even so gracious as to throw in a nonrequested sign for extra encouragement (see Judg. 7:13–15).

Again we ask ourselves, "Should we follow Gideon's methods as a prescriptive example of how to discern God's will?" There are no indications in this context that others are to use these methods. Subsequent Scripture passages contain no illustrations of the same procedures nor are there any references to this event as a model. Then why would we view Gideon's behavior as anything other than descriptive of this one-time event?

Statements with Guidance Terminology

A number of passages in the Old Testament use terms such as *guide, direct, instruct,* and *seek*. These texts are sometimes transferred, by a surface reading, into advice about how to know God's will. The use of these verses often depends on using the King James Version since later translations have chosen different words to translate the Hebrew. Be aware that many "will of God" stereotypes are tied to the King James translation. Modern translations have often changed the wording. These often-slight substitutions of words can make a lot of difference in how a verse is perceived in a surface reading. Let's examine some examples.

Proverbs 3:5–6 is a classic example of an illegitimate transfer of surface language into our culture without regard for the original context.

> Trust in the LORD with all thine heart;
> and lean not unto thine own understanding.

In all thy ways acknowledge him, and
he shall direct thy paths.

Proverbs 3:5–6 KJV

The stereotypical reading of this passage is that if we abandon trying to figure life out ("lean not unto thine own understanding") and just trust and acknowledge who God is and that he loves and controls the world and our lives, then we will enjoy the direct guidance of God in our lives ("he shall direct thy paths"). It is assumed that this direction is some sort of direct information from God to us about what we should do in a given situation as a reward for our trusting him. There is also the subtle assumption that a mental vacuum is a principle of spirituality. This kind of reading of Proverbs 3 misses the teaching intent of the text and leads one into a subjective process of discernment. "Trust" becomes a "letting go and letting God have his way" kind of attitude, an attitude contrary to the biblical meaning of trusting God.

The kind of trust God requires and the direction he provides is clarified when the context of Proverbs 3 is understood. Proverbs 3:1–12 is one of a series of poems in chapters 1–9. This is a poem of "instructional wisdom," where the father is teaching the son regulations about life. Verses 1–2 set the tone:

My son, do not forget my teaching,
but keep my commands in your heart,
for they will prolong your life many years
and bring you prosperity.

The contextual tone is that the father is conveying his instructions from one generation to another. As Scripture, the father's teaching is equivalent to God's teaching. In 3: 3, the father selects two of the great Old Testament values, "love and faithfulness" (the NIV's translation of two key Hebrew terms literally meaning "covenant loyalty" and "truthfulness") as values providing principles of guidance that should be ever present with the son/believer. Trust, in this context, is understood to be our belief that God's revelation about how to live is superior to any of our own constructs. When we make God's teaching preeminent, then "he will make your paths straight" (3:6 NIV) in the sense that God's truth shows the way. The moral teaching of this section of Proverbs is not something that the Old Testament believer had to find. It was already established in previous divine teaching. Here it is restated as the father passes his wisdom to the son.

Terms of guidance in the Old Testament assume the text of the Old Testament as the content of guidance. Psalm 23:3, "He guides me in paths of righteousness for his name's sake," asserts that God's law, which constitutes the "paths of righteousness," is the life direction God provides. Psalm 25 is particularly full of guidance terminology. Terms like *show, guide, teach,* and *instruct* permeate the psalm.

> Show me your ways, O LORD,
>   teach me your paths;
> guide me in your truth and teach me,
>   for you are God my Savior,
>   and my hope is in you all day long.
> Remember, O LORD, your great mercy and love,
>   for they are from of old.
> Remember not the sins of my youth
>   and my rebellious ways;
> according to your love remember me,
>   for you are good, O LORD.
> Good and upright is the LORD;
>   therefore he instructs sinners in his ways.
> He guides the humble in what is right
>   and teaches them his way.

All the ways of the LORD are loving and faithful
    for those who keep the demands of his covenant.
For the sake of your name, O LORD,
    forgive my iniquity, though it is great.
Who, then, is the man that fears the LORD?
    He will instruct him in the way chosen for him.
He will spend his days in prosperity,
    and his descendants will inherit the land.
The LORD confides in those who fear him;
    he makes his covenant known to them.

verses 4–14

How are these pleas of David to be understood? Is he requiring further revelation from God about the specifics of his life situation in order to be successful? Is David looking for something he has failed to find in order to live a life pleasing to God? No, David uses religious language to reflect upon life's struggle and concludes that the covenant God who has taught his children his ways is the only hope for moral knowledge and the will to obey. When you pursue God's covenant truth, you develop a moral integrity and uprightness that will bring you victory in the midst of life's struggle (Ps. 25:21). The very character of God—love, goodness, uprightness, covenant faithfulness—makes up the moral traits David sees as his need (vv. 4–5), as possessed by God (vv. 6–8), and as conveyed by God to those who obey him (vv. 9–15).

God addressed David's struggle by showing him that life is *in* his Word, not apart from it. As in many of the psalms, David's complaint and plea turns to recognition and praise that God has already provided what he needed in terms of God's own character and promises. David did not need to look elsewhere but rather needed to engage what God had already revealed. Bible passages like Proverbs 3 and Psalm 25 are not to be read as pleas for, or promises of, additional revelatory guidance in the struggle of life. Rather, the writers bare their souls as wise teachers, dependent upon the character and instruction of God. Terms such as *show, teach, guide, direct, seek,* and *instruct* do not imply an immediate revelatory process of guidance. Rather, they are terms of exhortation within contexts that offer wisdom for life by moral and godly value development based on what God has already revealed. When Psalm 73:24 states, "You guide me with your counsel, and afterward you will take me into glory," it is asserting that the whole cycle of life is lived in light of God's Word. It cannot be read with the assumption that the "counsel" of God is achieved through a means other than Scripture (cf. Prov. 2:4–6; 8:17; 9:10).

When Isaiah stated, "Your ears will hear a voice behind you, saying, 'This is the way; walk in it'" (30:21), he was not promoting an immediate voice of God for guidance. Rather, he was looking off to a future day when the truth of God and its teachers would be unhindered so that any deviation from God's Word would bring immediate conviction. When we ask the question in our own day, "What should I do?" God's Word still wants to respond, "This is the way, and these are the values that should guide your actions."

Reading the New Testament

We have already observed how the phrase "will of God" is developed in the New Testament. The sovereign and moral will of God dominates passages where there is a direct reference to this subject. Commands to acquire knowledge of God's will in the New Testament are similar to those of the Old Testament—a call to engage the teaching of the Bible and the apostles up to that point in time. Now we will consider New Testament stories and events to see how believers pursued God's will. We will also consider the question of how supernatural guidance was experienced in the New Testament and what that means for Christians today.

Jesus' Example of Pursuing God's Will

Psalm 40, quoted in Hebrews 10:57 and applied to the earthly life of Christ, summarizes Christ's example of doing God's will:

> Therefore, when Christ came into the world, he said:
> "Sacrifice and offering you did not desire,
>> but a body you prepared for me;
> with burnt offerings and sin offerings
>> you were not pleased.
> Then I said, 'Here I am—it is written about me in the scroll—
>> I have come to do your will, O God.'"

The reference to God's will here is a classic example that God's plan is God's will. Jesus was unique, of course, but he became a man under the messianic expectations of the Old Testament. How did he fulfill those expectations? Did he have to figure out what doing God's will meant? Did he have to find it? No. He merely obeyed God's Word with the special application of being its fulfillment! As Hebrews 5:8–9 states, "Although he was a son, he learned obedience from what he suffered and, once made perfect, he became the source of eternal salvation for all who obey him." Even for Jesus, character development was at the core of doing God's will.

Jesus fulfilled God's will by submitting to the sovereign plan and exemplifying the moral expectations of Scripture. He was born in Bethlehem in fulfillment of Micah 5:2. He consciously lived out the purposes of the Servant of the Lord (Luke 4:14–30). He fulfilled the plan of God by his choices (Matt. 3:13–17; John 4:34). He promoted conformity to God's moral will to those who followed his teaching (Mark 3:35; Matt. 7:21; John 7:16–17; 9:31). He sought the teaching of Scripture to deal with the issues of life that confronted him (Matthew 4:1–11; 5:17–20; chapters 5–7). Furthermore, Jesus expected the Jewish people to whom he was sent to know what the Bible expected and act on it (John 3; 5:39–40; Luke 24:25–27). He insisted that those who possessed the Bible not only obey its explicit teaching but also reason out the implications of its teaching and values in life's circumstances (Matthew 23:23; chapters 5–7; cf. 2 Cor. 3:6). For Jesus, to live under and flesh out God's plan and moral teaching was the substance of doing God's will.

Jesus passed his teaching to the apostles so that they could pass it on to the next generation (Matt. 28:18–20). The apostles understood Jesus' teaching as crucial and they in turn taught what they had received without reduction (2 Tim. 2:2).

Examples in the Book of Acts

As in the Old Testament, the New Testament contains examples of God using supernatural means to lead his people. Acts provides the most direct examples of supernatural guidance as it chronicles the history of the early church from Jerusalem to Rome and points beyond. The book focuses on key people and events in this phase of redemptive history, telling the story from the divine perspective of the Holy Spirit's work in the spread of the church.

The last biblical reference to the ancient practice of lot casting to make a decision is presented in Acts 1:21–26.

Two candidates were presented to fill the apostolic position abandoned by Judas. Matthias was chosen. This is the first and last mention of Matthias in the Bible. This event is typical of the lot-casting method. A choice was made among qualified options and then viewed as God's sovereign will.

Several events in Acts were directly orchestrated by God. God initiates these events as his redemptive work in the world unfolds. These examples do not fit a model of seeking knowledge to make a decision but once again illustrate God's sovereign control over the development of his plan. The major events include the following:

Philip and the Ethiopian (Acts 8:26–40)

Saul's conversion (Acts 9)

Ananias (Acts 9:10–19)

Peter's vision (Acts 10)

Agabus's prophesy of famine (Acts 11:27–30)

Peter's escape from prison (Acts 12)

Barnabas and Saul (Acts 13:1–3) . . . and aspects of Paul's missionary journeys

Were these examples intended to be normative models for future believers in understanding divine guidance? Is the Book of Acts prescribing how we should operate or is it describing what happened in that time frame? Acts is a story, not a manual; it is primarily descriptive rather than prescriptive. We see no mandates to duplicate the methods within the Book of Acts, merely the story of how the church began to fulfill the Great Commission given by Jesus (Matt. 28:18–20).

Understanding narrative examples as descriptive is a normal way to read Acts. At the same time, God communicated with his people in supernatural ways during this period (see 1 Corinthians 12–14). This is an element of the continuing revelation that was part of the apostolic period. The continuation or cessation of direct revelatory processes is a matter of debate in the church. I believe we no longer enjoy direct revelation as a part of God's method of guidance.

The Apostles' Example of Knowing God's Will

We observed in chapter 5 that the New Testament's teaching about God's will is focused on the sovereign and moral aspects. Exhortations to know God's will are calls to relate to the information already disseminated, not something yet to be discovered. The apostles continued to model dependence upon past revelation. They taught the church to judge the accuracy of their teaching on the basis of whether it passed the test of time. Peter and Paul merely perpetuated what they had received from authoritative tradition (2 Peter 1:19–21; 1 Cor. 15:1–11; cf. Luke 1:1–4; 2 Tim. 3:15–17; 1 Cor. 10:1–13), and they expected those they taught to do the same (2 Thess. 2:15; 2 Tim. 2:2; 2 Peter 3:15–16). The content of this teaching and its derived values constituted God's will for those who heard and obeyed.

The apostles' standard operating procedure for the pursuit of God and godliness was to live out the Word of God they had received. They expected their followers to do the same. Neither Jesus nor the apostles left us a paradigm for knowing God's will through a subjective process to figure out what God requires. Rather, they modeled living and making decisions on the basis of applying God's truth to their world. The process is bathed in prayer and submission to God's sovereign plan. A search for knowledge about the future in order to make a decision in the present is absent in apostolic instruction. Paul's final letters, the Pastoral Epistles (1 and 2 Timothy and Titus), present a paradigm of sound doctrine and judgment as the basis of discernment. No model of an appeal to miraculous guidance is present.

Conclusion

Learning to live by biblical teaching is more challenging than locating specific verses to address our questions. We must develop a biblical worldview and values set that represents the depth and breadth of Scripture. We must develop our skills to discern the direct and implied levels of biblical teaching. We need to understand the creative theological constructs of our personal religious traditions so that we can discern which level of biblical teaching we are evaluating. We must also learn to distinguish when the Bible is describing redemptive history and when it is prescribing normative patterns.

The Bible contains numerous examples of supernatural guidance in the fulfillment of God's will. These events, however, are relatively rare in the bigger picture and are always connected to unique persons or circumstances within the unfolding plan of God. They describe how God has acted and do not prescribe how God *will* act. As the Bible progresses in its teaching, the paradigm of dependence upon biblical truth and its values as the content of knowing and doing God's will predominates. The normative teaching is obedience to God's instructions to fulfill his will.

Jesus and the apostles modeled an absolute dependence on God and their inherited redemptive history. They were also part of a continuing process of special revelation. Yet when the content is evaluated, surprisingly little is totally new in the overall pool of knowledge. What is new relates primarily to the first climax of the messianic program in Christ's advent and the role of the church in God's sovereign plan. The focus is on promises fulfilled and the continuing need for obedience to God's moral will.

Consequently, when I obey the teaching of the Bible, I am doing God's will. As I continue to live for God by means of a transformed mind that applies biblical values, I am assured of his guidance. This guidance is not in response to my demand for information ahead of time in order to make a sound decision. Rather, his teaching is the guidance. Discernment of the issues of life is not to be suspended until some yet unrevealed information has surfaced. Instead, we must deal with these issues from a biblical worldview and values set. As we walk in God's ways, leaning on his values and not our own, we can rest in the fact that his truth will direct our paths. This is the way of Proverbs 3 and Romans 12.

What about Bob?   7

Becoming an Adult Decision Maker

■ One of the funniest movies I've seen was *What about Bob?* Bob Wiley, played by Bill Murray, was a psychiatrist's worst nightmare. His paranoia made him absolutely dependent upon his counselor. Bob could not make any decision without talking to Dr. Marvin, and even after a chat he began to doubt what he had been told. Consequently, Dr. Leo Marvin, played by Richard Dreyfuss, was subject to Bob's needs seven days a week, twenty-four hours a day. Dr. Marvin even wrote a book called *Baby Steps,* in which he detailed how one should order his or her life. Bob, however, was unable to follow the book's instructions. He needed to hear the doctor's soothing and confirming voice for every situation he faced. After the good doctor and his family left for their lake home for a vacation, Bob had a crisis, located the doctor, and wormed his way into the hearts of the family in order to manipulate the doctor to meet his needs. Bob became the most lovable nuisance in history. He won the affection of the Marvin family, except for the good doctor, and finally managed to capture the doctor's undivided attention by marrying his sister!

Most Christians read a book about knowing God's will because they long to please God and live a safe and happy life at the same time. The stereotype of God's will in much of American Christian culture promises that both of these longings can be met if we find the center of God's will. Thus, finding God's will becomes the key to avoiding the mistakes that cause us pain. Like Bob, we have become obsessed with having Dr. Marvin (God) direct or confirm every action we take. We focus on a search rather than on following the instructions the doctor has already given us.

The stereotypical view of God's will in Christian culture is flawed. We have imagined that God's will is a private matter between God and us as individuals. We have naively adopted the mindset of Western culture and placed ourselves at the center of God's work in the world. We have ignored the clear teaching of the Bible that God's will is comprised of his revealed truth and instead have substituted a search for God's will over a path of obedience in what we already know. Therefore, we paralyze ourselves by searching for a phantom of our own making.

A careful read of the Bible presents a different view of the meaning of God's will. Neither the Old Testament nor the New Testament presents a model of living that requires finding some secret plan of God and learning how we fit into that plan before we can make any decision. We should be concerned instead with what God has already revealed. What has not been revealed is not our business (Deut. 29:29). We can trust God to fulfill his sovereign plan. We have arrogantly assumed that if God knows the future, he is bound to guide us through that maze. Such an assumption is driven by self-interest, no matter how piously we may state it.

The model of God's will that we do find in the Bible is clearly focused on the sovereign and moral will. God has an overall plan for his creation within a time and space continuum, which is part of his sovereign nature and prerogatives. Creation has no on-demand access to this plan. We know God's plan when he chooses to reveal it or when we see it fulfilled. On the other hand, the moral will of God is clearly aimed at the regulation of God's creation, dictating human responsibility. God's moral will is first contained in the command and exhortation structures of Scripture and is recorded in the Bible and the Bible alone. His moral will is derived secondarily by the implications of these structures. God's moral will is designed to guide the attitudes and behavior of his subjects.

The Bible reflects that God has directly and miraculously communicated his will to select persons in the flow of biblical history. The manner of this communication is best understood as describing God's actions, not prescribing repeatable methods of communication.

The reader at this point might ask, "What about decisions for which I cannot locate a direct command to guide me? Am I to assume that an almighty God cannot respond to my plight? Am I to assume that my concerns to know how to deal with what is not directly revealed will go unanswered?" No. The question is not *whether* God can respond but *how* has he planned to do so. This is the crux of our struggle; we must grapple with our understanding of God's Word and life as we know it. I believe that at this juncture we have the greatest opportunity to glorify God and fulfill his purpose of creating us in his image.

The Relationship of God's Will and Godly Discernment

Consider for a moment the possibility that we have created a concept of knowing God's will after our own notions and expectations. The result is that we look to God to do for us what he never intended to do. The typical presentation of God's will in many circles brings with it two assumptions: (1) that God requires us to find his plan for our lives in order to make life decisions and (2) that God will perform some kind of revealing act in order to communicate his will for our individual lives. These assumptions lead us down the wrong road. God has a different plan to care for us in this life, one to maximize the fact that he created us to be his image bearers under the umbrella of his declared will. We all struggle with the fact that heaven seems to be silent at the most inopportune times. Ironically, our naive spirituality leads us to dismiss or bury our feelings of anger and discouragement about that silence rather than ask why God is not responding to our call. We end up living lives of Christian "quiet desperation" and miss the journey God planned for us. How sad. We need to get the message that God has ordained our struggle in order to mature us in his image and help us deal with life. We confront these challenges by discerning how a biblical worldview and values set apply to life's decisions.

In a very real way, where God's revealed will ends, godly discernment begins (see figure 10). Godly discernment begins with the foundation of God's moral will as revealed in the Bible and continues as we develop transformed minds. For instance, the teaching intent of God's direct command not to commit adultery is clear. Jesus took this teaching intent to the next level by locating adultery as first in the mind, the seat of human intention. Jesus' theological analysis, "Don't even think about it," of the direct moral command "Do not commit adultery" opens new vistas of values that a mere external command did not.

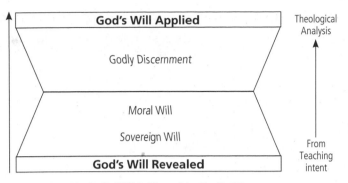

Fig. 10. God's Will Is Found in Godly Discernment

Reflect for a moment on the biblical command to love, the greatest of all commands according to Jesus. How do you factor love into your godly discernment of God's will? The term *love* is a "logical construct," an abstract term that is not self-defining as are terms like *chair, rock, girl,* and *boy.* How do you know the loving thing to do? Discerning the meaning of "Love God and love your neighbor" requires critical thinking about how to fulfill God's command.

The fact that God wants Christians to move to a new level of moral reflection is illustrated by the very terms that describe the Christian life. Paul and Peter give us major lists of Christian qualities that are to guide our lives.

The Fruit of the Spirit	Christian Virtue List
Love	Goodness
Joy	Knowledge
Peace	Self-Control
Patience	Perseverance
Kindness	Godliness
Goodness	Brotherly Kindness
Faithfulness	Love
Gentleness	(2 Peter 1:5–8)
Self-Control	
(Gal. 5:22–23)	

Most of these terms are *logical constructs* that solicit broad description rather than simple concrete definition. For example, you cannot draw a picture of love or joy or peace or kindness. As terms of Christian virtue, they need to be described by thinking about how such terms represent biblical values. Consequently, pursuing the Christian life brings with it the responsibility to grow in our ability to understand the deepest levels of virtue that a biblical worldview promotes.

You can see that godliness is not just correlation with a direct command. Jesus made it clear that one can abstain from committing adultery physically while still doing it mentally. One can maintain the appearance of outward conformity to Christian teaching while being a wreck on the inside. Godliness is the living out of the external command because of internal motivation. God can teach us to respect people and be kind, but the extension of these basic commands into the acts of life makes us godly.

Godly discernment in reference to God's will is what wisdom is in reference to knowledge. Wisdom is a product of knowledge. Discernment is a product of applying what we can know about God's will. Since discernment is a product, there must be a process to produce it. The process is found in Romans 12:12: Be transformed by the renewing of your mind. When the mind is renewed, it is then able to evaluate life from a new perspective. It is empowered to apply a biblical worldview and values set to everyday decisions. This is part of what Jesus meant when he distinguished between the letter and spirit of the law.

There is no decision or issue in life that is not addressed by biblical values. We sometimes believe the Bible is silent on some issues. We think this, however, because our minds are too small and our discipline of drawing truth from Scripture too unpracticed. On the other hand, we will experience a lack of absolute proof for some of our decisions. We will also experience a variance in the understanding of discernment within the greater Christian community. Yet God allows the diversity in order to achieve a greater goal than mere uniformity. We live now with unity in diversity. This is God's plan. This is the reality we know.

So what are you as a decision maker to do? "Study, make every effort, to show yourself approved unto God, a workman that does not need to be ashamed, correctly handling the word of truth" (2 Tim. 2:15, author's paraphrase).

Developing Discernment Skills

If the core of God's will is Scripture's record of God's sovereign and moral will, then discernment consists in the application of our understanding how God's revealed will applies to our decisions. You are not responsible to find God's will; you are responsible to do what he has told you to do and to develop a biblical sense of what to do when there is no clear direct teaching. Discernment takes the various levels of biblical teaching—direct, implied, and creative constructs—and develops a worldview and values mindset to interpret the decisions of life.

Foundations for Discerning God's Will

You can find a book about God's will that says exactly what you want to hear if you look long enough. You have to decide, however, which view really reflects biblical teaching and is a sound evaluation of the way God has designed life to work. Let's review the common approaches to knowing God's will. If you are interested in exploring this in more detail, please see the bibliography at the end of this book.

The common themes in the literature on what it means to know God's will include:

know the Bible
live a godly life
pray
know yourself thoroughly
learn to hear the divine voice
be alert to circumstances
seek wise counsel
no matter what, make decisions!

These items represent areas of concern by all who propose models for knowing and doing God's will. Each author expands upon the issues internal to each category and how these items coalesce to lead one to God's will. Interestingly, authors of diverse theological understandings use the same categories! They merely apply their own presuppositions to how they explain each category. The most controversial category is "learn to hear the divine voice." One author might argue that God is still doing a work of direct revelation. Another might talk about impressions and "holy hunches" from the Holy Spirit. Others understand God's voice as the consensus of the community. I would assert that the "voice" this category represents is the objective voice of God's Word that informs our worldview and values and is the base of the Spirit's conviction.

Interestingly, all views admit a certain level of uncertainty in knowing absolutely the divine mind unless they posit direct revelation. Yet even then, everyone else is uncertain about how they prove it! The result is that you, the reader, are left with a lot of advice about what you should think about, but you discover that you are still chewing on an Almond Joy candy bar when you come right down to the moment of decision—you are still left with the "indescribable." This is because most models are more subjective than objective in how they process the data.

I believe that all of these categories contribute to godly discernment, but a larger umbrella determines their validity—biblical worldview and values. This umbrella gives coherence to the variety of categories and makes judgments about the contribution of each in any given situation. In making a decision, each category must pass the test of our worldview and values set, which is the filter that makes judgments about everything you contemplate. You should be able to state these reasons objectively on a piece of paper and thereby say, "This is why I have decided to do this." You can confidently affirm that you are taking the right and appropriate course of action even though you do not know what the future will bring in light of your decision. Your confidence is grounded in applying biblical truth to life's events. Even when you discover that things are not turning out as you imagined they would, you can point to the values that drove your decision and cling to your course of action regardless of where it leads you. Is it not amazing that in spite of circumstances and the advice of others, Job never abandoned his worldview about God and his circumstances? An objective criterion helped him stay the course in the midst of pain and suffering, enabling him to fulfill God's sovereign plan and learn lessons he could never have learned in more pleasant pastures.

I stated earlier that I believe we have operated under some false assumptions about what it means to know God's will. We have assumed that we are supposed to tap in to God's all-knowing telephone line and discern the future in order to make a decision. Doing so guarantees that we are "in God's will" rather than "out of God's will," which is the consequence of not finding it. I believe this is a flawed assumption and that it leads us to presume upon God's sovereign will and makes demands upon God that he has never promised to meet. Rather, God expects his image bearers to engage the challenges of life and make decisions in light of the worldview and values system the Bible teaches. God is glorified by his creation when we do this. God will oversee his sovereign plan while we fulfill our responsibility to do what Jesus would do to the best of our ability. We do this in submission to God. We do this in an atmosphere of godly living that is bathed in prayer. We fulfill our roles, with all the ups and downs, with full confidence that God will fulfill his plan for his world and us.

Developing a Discernment Process

I would suggest four steps to follow in Christian discernment. You need to (1) know the Bible, (2) develop a Christian worldview, (3) identify your values, and (4) apply a decision-making process. These steps will ultimately include all of the categories of concern mentioned above. In my model, however, all of these concerns are defined and exercised under the umbrella of a well-defined worldview and values set.

Know the Bible

Pursuing God's will on the basis of applying godly discernment drives us to a deeper and broader reading of the Bible. The reading is not deeper in the sense of finding some hidden meaning in the Bible, but in that we probe our understanding of the Bible more reflectively. The popular WWJD? (What would Jesus do?) jewelry illustrates what we mean by a deeper reading. Apart from clear moral commands, WWJD? is a hypothetical question to make us think like we think Jesus would think. This is a noble effort, but how would we know if we are thinking like Jesus? There is only one answer. We have to permeate our minds with the same information Jesus absorbed and applied in his own thinking patterns. The Old Testament supplies the ideas Jesus devoured. The Gospels provide the results of Jesus' assimilation of those ideas. The Epistles of the New Testament continue the accumulation of learning from Jesus' thinking. If we are going to take WWJD? seriously, then we must immerse our minds in the only literature that can prepare us to give a reasoned answer to the question WWJD? as it applies to the events of life.

Knowing the Bible is not simply the memorization of Bible verses. Because of the normative nature of much of biblical teaching, memorizing terse moral codes is useful. It is good to have "Do not lie" in our consciousness. Memorizing words without contextual understanding, however, does not adequately transform the mind. This procedure merely provides words that we apply in isolation from their context. If we miss the intended teaching of the passage, we may make a false claim upon the Bible and God. Such a practice can result in frustration and even anger. We pull out memory verses in times of crisis as if they were magical amulets to address our problems. When it does not work, who gets the blame? Such a practice may condition us to think that the Bible does not work or that God does not care.

DEVELOP A CHRISTIAN WORLDVIEW

As we described earlier in this book, a worldview is comprised of the basic beliefs we hold that give us a conceptual framework to interpret our world and ourselves.[1] A Christian worldview is one that is informed by biblical knowledge. It will address our beliefs about who we are (ontology), how we know what we know (epistemology), and what we value as acceptable behavior (axiology). A Christian worldview will account for these categories within the framework of the biblical story of creation, fall, redemption, and consummation.

As Christians, our worldview is controlled by the belief that God exists and that he has communicated to his creation and that the Bible is the only authoritative record of that communication. From this ultimate presupposition, we develop numerous beliefs that guide our lives. We affirm that our world and ourselves are the direct creation of God. This truth guides our thinking about the uniqueness of planet Earth, the human body and soul, and the purpose of existence. These beliefs yield ideas about how to treat our world and the people in it. Issues of cloning, cell research, capital punishment, euthanasia, earth and animal rights, management and labor relations, an understanding of our humanness as males or females, and all other subjects are affected by our beliefs.

We affirm the truth of the Genesis story about Adam's sin and how that is interpreted throughout the Bible. This belief addresses the problem of evil in our world and ourselves. Understanding how Eden affected us helps us deal with our limitations. We view the story of God's redemptive work as central to the history of our world. This belief affirms that history is guided by a divine plan and that this life is not the totality of human existence. God will bring earth history to a consummation. How we understand God's control of his world forms our views of the role of prayer. These beliefs and many more influence our understanding of all of the areas that we evaluate in our process of making everyday decisions.

When you are in touch with your worldview and values system, you are better prepared to weigh the information you surface in the decision-making process. If you have not thoroughly evaluated the issue you face in light of biblical teaching, you will be convicted to do so. You will come to realize the necessary exercise of the spiritual disciplines of godly living, prayer, and meditation. These disciplines are not performed to acquire a revelation about a decision. Nor are they a means of manipulating God. Their purpose is to keep you centered on God's moral will as he fulfills his sovereign plan. You will be respectful of the circumstances and timing of life's events, because you know that God is in control of your world. You will learn to listen and weigh the advice of friends because you know that you cannot see yourself as others see you. You will not be paralyzed by the fear of making decisions, because you know that even failure is an opportunity for God to help you grow in your understanding of how to live. You will realize that what you and others may view as failure may be the very plan God designed to conform you to the image of Christ.

This book cannot communicate everything you need to know about becoming a good decision maker. You must take the journey yourself. In the journey, you learn what no book can tell you. As the proverb states, "You can give a person a fish and feed him for the day, or you can teach him how to fish and feed him forever." My hope is that I offer you some new perspectives on what it means to think "Christianly" so that you can take the journey yourself.

IDENTIFY YOUR VALUES

I once heard a preacher say, "Before I was a Christian, I loved things and used people. Now that I am a Christian, I love people and use things." This simple statement speaks volumes about values. We previously noted that values operate at three levels: biblical commands, community, and personal. All Christians value what the Bible commands. A command not to lie reflects the value of truth telling. A command not to commit adultery values human relationships. A command to love, however, is more difficult to describe. Love is presented throughout Scripture as the ultimate value in human relationships. Love is a command that not only is direct but also permeates community values. We are constantly challenged to determine what it is to do the loving thing. Personal values include our tastes in food, music, entertainment, use of free time, and everything about our lives that we control. Sit down sometime and draw up your list of values for these three levels, especially community and personal.

Apply a Decision-Making Process

Daily we confront a myriad of issues about which we must make decisions and act upon those decisions. For me, it could be something as mundane as whether to pack a lunch or eat out with my colleagues. While this seems simple, it is driven by values and consequences. For example, can I afford to eat out? Lunch with tip will cost seven to eight dollars. Not a big deal, unless I do it every day, then the budget begins to feel it. If I spend my money here, will I lack funds to take my wife and/or children out sometime during the week? Whom do I value most? If I value both, how do I balance those commitments? How does my family view my actions? Am I developing patterns of selfishness? Or perhaps I have a mound of student papers to grade and I should not take sixty to ninety minutes away from my desk. But grading is a pain, so go out! But then at the end of the week, the papers are still there and not returned in a timely manner. Then I am forced to work on Saturday when no one is in the office building and no temptations exist to detract me from my grading. But then I have destroyed key family time by the decisions I made during the week.

Does God have a will in all of this? I think so. It is a will that is found in the reflection and application of values that reflect godly living. The process that addresses this common scenario is the same as that which addresses "Whom should I marry?" "What career should I pursue?" "Where should I give my money?" "What church should I attend?" "Should I change jobs?" "Should I be an usher or a deacon?" The so-called major decisions need the clarification of options and values just like the decisions of a typical day.

One of the first disciplines of decision making is to develop a pattern of linking our values to the decisions that confront us. This must become a mental habit. It can be very threatening because we all have values that are less than noble. The truly self-conscious person is able to deal with the bad as well as the good values. We must raise the integrity of our self-consciousness to a new level if we are serious about knowing and doing God's will. As a teacher, I often struggle with the drudgery of grading. I read my students' papers. I believe I owe them that courtesy. I have been accused of being a workaholic (not a good value or something to be proud of), but I humor myself with how creative I can become to avoid certain tasks! This fact confronts us with the functions of conscience and our own will. The role of conscience will be addressed in the next chapter of this book.

The decision-making chart (see figure 7 on page 65) is one method to help us process decisions in reference to our worldview and values set. The rectangular box contains a list of categories that stimulate relating values to the questions that call for discernment. The list is only suggestive and will vary in its items and focus depending on the issues under consideration. No order of priority is intended in the way these items are presented. Reflect with me about how these items can engage the decision-making process.

The need for a high level of *critical self-awareness* is crucial if we are to be godly decision makers. Knowing ourselves may be our greatest challenge. The heart, that is, the mind, is deceitful and desperately wicked; who can know it? (Jer. 17:9). *I* am the first one who meets each issue that calls for discernment in my life. *I* am the one who decides whether to obey a biblical value and how far to press the borders. *I* am the one who knows what is right when I do what is wrong (see Romans 7). I need to probe myself to uncover the sinful strategies I use to control my world. I need to know what drives me as a person. My blind sides, or the areas about which I have not gained self-awareness, will color my decisions. How can I, how can you, work to achieve deeper levels of self-understanding? There's an old country song with a line that says, "I got twenty-twenty vision, but I'm walkin' 'round blind!"

Two life-changing experiences have helped raise my own level of self-awareness. A few months after being discharged from the navy, I received a packet in the mail—my entire military file, all of my records from four years of service. Included in this packet were all of the confidential written reviews of my supervisors during that period. It was an eye-opener! They contained candid statements about my strengths and weaknesses, put my personal traits on the table for inspection, pointed out patterns I knew I had but had never really seen through the eyes of another person. The perspectives of second and third parties helped me see myself as others see me. While I knew some of my traits, I never really saw how I applied them in social and work settings. Reading these reviews opened vistas of self-understanding that I would never have probed on my own. This is the value of a community that is honest with its members. This is easy to achieve in the military where superiors can speak honestly about those over whom they have control. However, it is not so easy to achieve in a family or a church where everyone wears their feelings on their sleeves and never forgets the negative evaluative words of others. When was the last time you sat down for coffee with a close friend and asked him or her to dismantle you without holding back? If you have ever been asked this question, and few have, you probably held back because you didn't know how to deal with such intimidating scrutiny.

The second life experience that raised my self-awareness was one such sit-down coffee session. I had the privilege of meeting with about six experienced and high-powered colleagues every two weeks over the period of a year. Our lives were exposed, unpacked, and evaluated in an atmosphere of real love. True love is not the superficial "you're wonderful" scenario. True love is the ability to be honest about hard things so that we can move to another level of self-understanding. In fact, without this kind of community, you will never know what I am talking about.

The Bible also says a great deal about *human obligations*. It addresses the responsibilities we maintain in family and world relationships. Fathers, mothers, parents, unmarried persons, children, children to aging parents, husbands, wives, masters and servants (needing cultural adaptation for the categories of employer and employee), and communities of persons are addressed in great detail throughout Scripture. As we move on the continuum of our human responsibilities, the rules under which we operate have to adjust. Certain decisions we make as single persons cannot be evaluated in the same way if we are married with children. Changing obligations bring changing values. The

Bible maintains a high standard of human responsibility in all of our social relationships. Many decisions require analysis from this perspective.

The *providence of God* is an aspect of God's sovereignty. Providence is a creative concept that represents the biblical teaching about God working out his purposes in the world. Our lives are part of that work. Providence is an active rather than a passive concept. As the cliché goes, "God moves in mysterious ways, his wonders to perform." Our role in godly discernment is to be sensitive to the circumstances of life in which we find ourselves. Because we assume that God is in control of our world, we should therefore assume that where we find ourselves circumstantially is God's will. This assumes, of course, that our circumstantial setting is within God's moral will. The timing of decisions is important since providence is a part of the unfolding of history. For example, some years ago I was in the middle of a job change. It was going a bit slow. One good opportunity developed, and after careful evaluation, my family and I decided I should take the position. A week later I had about four phone calls with opportunities I might have preferred if I evaluated them. But we felt that the timing was crucial in these events and continued on our initial track. In other circumstances, the providence of timing might not be as much of an issue, but it was key in this setting.

Missionaries often face major decisions about God's will for their lives. The *researched opinion* of their mission board is often very influencing, if not directive, in regard to their service. I have often heard missionary couples explain how they had changed their minds from one field to another. Their explanation was often difficult, because they were trying to think out loud about how to deal with what they thought was a change in God's mind. If they felt called to one field but then changed direction, was that not a change on God's part? I think a good deal of this kind of stress is based on false assumptions of how they decided on a field in the first place. A first choice is often based more on emotional than reasoned response—friends served on that field, a certain speaker was totally captivating. There may be any number of influencing settings. These settings are usually part of God's providence to draw persons into vocational Christian service. But the development of their calling geographically is usually subject to the researched opinion of the needs and opportunities of world evangelism at any given time in history. Godly discernment pays attention to these details and assumes that this is part of God's guidance. Researched opinion also applies to the church in its global presence.

Christians must grapple with how they view their *roles and obligations in God's kingdom.* All believers are charged with basic Christian responsibilities. But our roles within the church will vary. The body imagery, offices, and functions described in the New Testament make it clear that we each have a role to fulfill. Our placement in these roles is based on our desires exercised under God's sovereign control and is accomplished by the church as a community recognizing and approving who does what. Once we understand our roles, the values that come with our responsibilities form a part of the discernment process.

The most difficult area of discernment for sincere Christians relates to *our personal desires.* Believers often struggle with how to relate what they do not like to do and what they enjoy. I have often heard believers say, "Oops, I better not say that I will not do that or that is what God will make me do!" Or "I really want to do this, but I'm afraid that my desires may detract from knowing what God wants." I am not sure why Christians often feel that God is looking for opportunities to make them unhappy. Perhaps this perception is self-induced, assuming that because we are sinners, we can never trust our feelings. I am sure that this is not a good view of the nature of God. I certainly do not find the psalmists or other believers in the Bible reflecting this kind of attitude. Or if they do, like Elijah (1 Kings 19), God certainly corrects them. Furthermore, personal desire is the nature of the call to pastoral ministry (1 Tim. 3:1).

We need to know what we really like, because that is a window to what drives our motivation in life. This is an important aspect of our self-awareness. We will skew our values if we do not acknowledge our personal desires. We are often so concerned about externalism and meeting the expectations of others that we neglect knowing ourselves. Religion, by its own nature in the human arena, thrives on the expectation of external conformity and often squelches personal desire. We need to tap in to what makes us happy and channel those energies into divine service. We may often give other values higher priority and choose to do the hard and less enjoyable tasks, but we must do so knowing why. Understanding our own motivations is the key to value clarification in discernment.

Some years ago I was standing with my faculty colleagues in a commencement line waiting to march in our graduation exercises. I forget the exact nature of our conversation, but I remember a question a friend of mine asked: "What makes you happy?" It seems simple enough. But as I thought about it, I could not give an easy answer. Sure, ice cream, banjo music, sunshine, family, friends, and resources to enjoy the good things of life all make me happy. But my friend was not seeking a superficial answer. What were the deepest longings of my soul? I still think about that question daily.

One of the most neglected aspects of discernment in American culture is how to tap *the wisdom of a community*. Americans are fiercely independent. We can do it on our own. We view *ourselves* as the most important ingredient in all of our situations. Western and American culture have bred such attitudes. American values rather than biblical ones often influence our thinking in this regard. The Bible emphasizes instead the believing *community*. God dealt with Israel as a nation. What affected one affected all. This community approach is also modeled in the New Testament. In our culture, we often image spiritual gifts as a personal quest. In the New Testament, however, the discovery and function of gifts was thoroughly stimulated by and integrated into a community environment. In our culture, spirituality is often thought of as a private matter between God and the individual. In the New Testament, however, the whole concept of spirituality was tied to the believing community relationships (see Galatians 5–6). The community dynamic in fulfilling God's will is often a missing characteristic in the Christian community. We need to learn to listen to how the community as a whole views each of us as individuals. We need to learn to listen to the judgment of the community about God's work in the world.

Conclusion

In this chapter, we have considered God's will in terms of applying godly discernment rather than trying to figure out God's sovereign plan in advance. There is no biblical model for the latter. When you try to make your decisions by searching for information about the future, you find yourself paralyzed by inaction or frustrated by a silent heaven. This is not the way God has taught us to pursue him and his will. God has called us, and the apostles have taught us, to live responsible lives in light of biblical teaching. This pattern is also observed in the Old Testament.

We have reviewed the ingredients that are common in all models that address knowing God's will. I believe that the information and insights of these items are all utilized under the four major categories of knowing your Bible, developing a Christian worldview, identifying your values, and practicing a process of evaluating the decisions that you make.

Before we look at some case studies that probe making decisions from your worldview and values set, we will explore several issues that pertain to the more subjective side of knowing God's will. Part 3 reviews the roles of conscience, the Holy Spirit, prayer, and other subjective issues in our efforts to discern God's will.

Subjective Challenges to Knowing God's Will

The first two parts of this book addressed the foundations and biblical patterns of knowing God's will. By now you should be wondering about all those little voices in your head. Who is talking to you? God? The devil? The Holy Spirit? Yourself? All of us experience constant voices within our minds. We are not suffering from multiple personalities; we are involved in a constant internal debate about what we see and hear. A movie flashes a suggestive or blatant sex scene. We didn't want to see it, but now we hear those voices. Voices of temptation. Voices of rationalization. Voices of critique. Perhaps you stopped at a gas station on the way to work and while you were pumping gas, you heard a voice, "Go over and witness to that guy pumping gas." Or when you got to work, you heard a voice saying, "Go to the president of your company and share your testimony now." Is this God's voice? Is this my guilty conscience speaking because I seldom witness? All believers are to be witnesses, but when, where, and how? If we immediately responded to every voice in our minds that instructs us to do something we know is good, would that voice advance our testimony or undermine it? Would our response prove our spirituality or make others think we are a few rocks short of a full load? What are we to do with these subjective voices and impressions?

The roles of the conscience and the Holy Spirit are major issues in godly discernment. We want to be obedient, but how do we know if these voices are directly from God and therefore require immediate obedience, or whether we are simply having an internal conversation with ourselves over values. What does the Bible say about the function of conscience and Spirit in our lives?

Apart from these two areas, we all experience a range of impressions that flash on the billboards of our minds. Do this! Don't do this! We have impressions of uneasiness over certain thoughts and decisions, while we claim peace over others. How do we evaluate these inner struggles?

What about God's will in terms of our vocation or service in the church? How do we know if we are "called" to a given task? What about prayer? Does prayer change things?

The following chapters will attempt to address these concerns and other areas that are "behind the veil" and therefore beyond our ability to verify.

8

The Role of Conscience

■ Sometimes I do my best self-reflection while driving. I'm sure I look a bit odd going down the highway talking to myself! Sometimes I even have to stop and take notes! Mowing the yard is another great time to think. Another time that my mind is plagued with self-reflection about life is when I quiet myself for prayer. When we try to shut out the world around us for reflection on God, the inner world of our minds surfaces all the business of life that we need to care for. The great Christian poet Frederick William Faber (1814–63) captured this experience wonderfully in the poem "Distractions in Prayer."

> Ah dearest Lord! I cannot pray,
> My fancy is not free;
> Unmannerly distractions come,
> And force my thoughts from Thee.
>
> The world that looks so dull all day
> Grows bright on me at prayer,

And plans that ask no thought but then
   Wake up and meet me there.

All nature one full fountain seems
   Of dreamy sight and sound,
Which, when I kneel, breaks up its deeps,
   And makes a deluge round.

Old voices murmur in my ear,
   New hopes start to life,
And past and future gaily blend
   In one bewitching strife.

My very flesh has restless fits;
   My changeful limbs conspire
With all these phantoms of the mind
   My inner self to tire.

I cannot pray; yet, Lord! Thou knowst
   The pain it is to me
To have my vainly struggling thoughts
   Thus torn away from Thee.

Sweet Jesus! Teach me how to prize
   These tedious hours when I,
Foolish and mute before Thy Face,
   In helpless worship lie.

Prayer was not meant for luxury,
   Or selfish pastime sweet;
It is the prostrate creature's place
   At his Creator's feet.

Had I, dear Lord! No pleasure found
   But in the thought of Thee,
Prayer would have come unsought, and been
   A truer liberty.

Yet Thou are oft most present, Lord!
   In weak distracted prayer:
A sinner out of heart with self
   Most often finds Thee there.

For prayer that humbles sets the soul
   From all illusions free,
And teaches it how utterly,
   Dear Lord! It hangs on Thee.

The heart, that on self-sacrifice
   Is covetously bent,
Will bless thy chastening hand that makes
   Its prayer its punishment.

My Saviour! Why should I complain
   And why fear aught but sin?
Distractions are but outward things;
   Thy peace dwells far within.

These surface-troubles come and go,
   Like rufflings of the sea;
The deeper depth is out of reach
   To all, my God, but Thee.

In such times of reflection, our minds race with conversations probing the ins and outs, pros and cons of whatever we are thinking about. Perhaps you remember someone you have offended. *I was in a bad mood when I put Judy down the other day. Now every time I see her, I know I should apologize. But why can't I take that first step?* Or you see someone at work who needs Christ and the voice comes to mind: *You need to witness to Joe.* You feel convicted to do so but then reflect on what it would mean for your work relationship. *He might not like me anymore. The work gang will start calling me "preacher." They know I am a Christian by the life that I live. Is that not enough?* Or you are riding down the road and see a sexually suggestive billboard. Thoughts pop into your mind. You immediately feel bad that you would have that thought and for the next ten miles you have a running debate in your consciousness about the incident. Then you crest the next hill and see the state trooper with his radar gun pointed at you and immediately feel convicted to hit the brakes since the cruise is set over the speed limit. You think, *I wish I could respond to moral conviction as quickly and decisively!* The trooper doesn't come after you and the word *grace* comes to mind.

How do we respond to this almost constant internal conversation? Do we think to ourselves, *Wow, I do not want to think this way.* Or do we entertain the thought for a while until a sense of guilt gets us back on track. We know that thoughts entertained too long are in danger of being born into acts. Yet we still find ourselves in constant battle with our inner reflections.

Where do all of these voices come from? Are we talking to ourselves? Or are these voices external, communicating to us through some sort of "chat room" in our minds? Understanding what constitutes the human conscience helps explain this internal experience.

Conscience in the Bible

Psychologists, philosophers, and theologians have various definitions and descriptions of what we call "conscience." Webster's dictionary informs us that the English word *conscience* is derived from the Latin word *conscientia,* meaning "joint or mutual knowledge." Webster defines *conscience* as "a knowledge or feeling of right and wrong, with a compulsion to do right; moral judgment that opposes the violation of a previously recognized ethical principle." Conscience is a vital part of one's self-awareness, since it fulfills a role of arbitration in moral discernment.

The Bible speaks little about conscience. There is no Hebrew word for conscience. The Greek term for it, like the Latin, is a term that means "to know with." As the usage of these terms developed, they came to depict an internal function of moral reflection, especially the pain one feels when secret and private knowledge becomes known or standards are violated. Interestingly, the Greek translation of the Old Testament, called the Septuagint, uses the noun only once (Eccles. 10:20) and the verb form twice (Lev. 5: 1; Job 27:6), although words for conscience were easily available. All three of these occurrences represent persons pursuing an internal critique of their thoughts.

There are about thirty uses of the noun *conscience* in the New Testament. Paul's Epistles take the lead with twenty-two, the Book of Hebrews has five, and 1 Peter contains three. Paul particularly engages the idea of conscience in 1 Corinthians (the term is used eleven times). It seems Paul developed his view of conscience through his interaction with the Corinthian church. From these passages we can draw the following definition and description. Conscience is a critical inner awareness, a *witness* in reference to the norms and values that we recognize and apply.[1] The conscience does not create norms and values but merely responds to our existing "software."

Conscience must be educated, programmed, in relation to a critically developed worldview and values set. Seeing conscience in this light amplifies the need to understand its function in Christian decision making—not as a judge but as a witness. A judge may render an original opinion, but a witness is confined to what he or she sees. A judge may render a decision, but a witness can only report. Values are the judge. Conscience merely witnesses life's decisions in light of the worldview and values set it has been programmed to use. The witness of conscience is sensed in terms of a conviction in relation to the subject contemplated. This conviction, however, is informed by our values system. Conscience is not an independent entity that gives us values but a function of our self-awareness to remind us of the values we recognize. Now, how would you react to the assertion, "Let your conscience be your guide"? I will give you my thoughts later in this chapter.

Conscience and values must be distinguished. To do so, consider figure 5 on page 47, which shows how our mind operates. When data comes to us to be evaluated, we run it through the grid of our worldview and values set. Our conscience relates the data to our values and alerts us when the data violates the values we recognize and apply. When conscience alerts us to a conflict of values, we must review our values set according to our understanding of God's Word. Conscience is, therefore, not an independent agent communicating information to us but a God-given self-reflective tool to keep us faithful to what we believe.

With this big picture in mind, let us review how the Bible refers to conscience.[2] These references give us several characteristics of the function of conscience in the New Testament. Conscience is first of all a capacity within our self-awareness for the purpose of self-critique. Paul makes a fascinating statement in 1 Corinthians 4:4: "My conscience is clear, but that does not make me innocent. It is the Lord who judges me." The New International Version rendering, "my conscience is clear," stands for the literal rendition, "I know nothing against myself." When Paul reflected on his relationship with the Corinthian believers, he could not surface one thought that condemned him or his actions. At the same time, he recognized that his own self-critique was limited. Conscience has its limitations. It can only relate to our own view of ourselves. Beyond that, we must answer to God. This clearly implies that conscience is not some direct voice of God that sends messages to us in spite of ourselves. To put it another way, the absence of conviction does not in itself justify an action.

If we are considering a thought or action, and our conscience does not give us a red light, are we free to pursue that thought or action? I think not. We must have reasons that justify our actions, not just good or bad feelings. Many times Christians will pursue a course of action because, as one might say, "My conscience does not prohibit me from doing this, therefore it cannot be wrong." This is an incorrect understanding of the role of that inner voice. Conscience is a servant of our values. If our values are wrong, we will not be convicted of wrongdoing but will naively assume we are okay. Our responsibility is to evaluate our values in light of the continuing transformation of our minds.

Romans 2:14–15 gives an interesting illustration of the capacity of conscience for self-critique. In Romans 1–3, Paul argues that both Jew and Gentile "have sinned and fall short of the glory of God" (3:23). The line of demarcation between the two groups is the possession of Moses' Law (2:12). Paul uses this single fact to heighten Jewish responsibility. Although the Gentiles sin without the guidance of the law, the Jews sin in spite of it. He uses this point illustratively in 2:14–15. For the Gentile, however, the conscience fulfilled the role of the law in that it convicted the Gentiles concerning their own values, which by common grace reflected the requirements of the law. These analogies to the law were "written on their hearts" (2:15). They, in contradistinction to the Jews, obeyed these ingrained principles under the conviction of their conscience, whereas the Jews, with the extra advantage of the law itself, only hardened their hearts. Consequently, for the Gentile, the conscience fulfilled a function of the law, the act of conviction in reference to values. Paul's use of the Gentiles as more consistent in moral self-critique than the Jews should have caused a sense of shame on the part of the privileged nation.

The conscience's capacity for self-critique is also noted by Paul's comment that the conscience can be seared (1 Tim. 4:2). The imagery of cauterizing is Paul's way of picturing a conscience that has been deprived of its function of self-critique. The inner awareness is no longer capable of sensing conviction. The references to a cauterized conscience (4:2) and the result of forbidding people to marry (4:3) are explanations of what it means to be a "hypocritical liar" (4:2). These liars have defrauded the "faith" (4:1), the teaching and values they once owned, and substituted false values. Since the role of conscience is to monitor our conformity to our values, if we violate those values, we have to find some way to make the conscience shut up.

The New Testament references to conscience present a second characteristic—conscience is a witness to the worldview and values system we recognize and apply. Paul appeals to the inner witness of the conscience in a number of settings. Please remember that in these contexts, the conscience is not the subject of Paul's reference but a witness to the subject being referenced. He notes that the conscience is an internal witness within Gentiles to monitor their moral value judgments (Rom. 2:15). Paul appeals to his own conscience as a witness that he has been upright in his ministry relationships (Rom. 9:1; 2 Cor. 1:12; cf. 1 Cor. 4:4). Paul also appeals to the conscience of others as an external witness to the validity of his ministry (2 Cor. 4:2; 5:11). In all of these cases, conscience is not an independent voice but a witness to an existing standard.

Another major use of conscience is observed when it is modified by adjectives like *good*, *clear*, and *pure* (1 Tim. 1:5; 1:19; 1 Peter 3:16, 21; 2 Tim. 1:3); *weak* (1 Cor. 8:7, 10, 12); and *evil* and *guilty* (Heb. 10:22). Each of these occurrences is similar to the witness feature of the conscience. The conscience testifies about the state of our mind by making a judgment in relation to a predetermined standard.

Paul gives us another interesting window into the use of conscience in 1 Corinthians 8–10. In these chapters Paul addresses a variety of problems that relate to the nature of the Greco-Roman culture. It was a society integrated with idolatry (Acts 17). The "idol's temple" (1 Cor. 8:10) was the social center of cities in this era. The temples provided for pagan worship as well as a place for multiple social functions. Archaeology has pointed out that the temples of the period contained numerous eating areas. Besides the cultic meals practiced in ancient religions, wedding parties and other social events probably convened in these spaces. Pagan temples and the Jewish synagogue system served as community centers for their respective constituencies. Paul's statements in 1 Corinthians reflect how the temple system was integrated into the food structures of a community. Meat and wine were routinely run through the temple system and eventually ended up in the open-air markets (10:25). Having meat in the markets that was "blessed" by the pagan priests was the norm, not the exception.

In 1 Corinthians, Paul was probably responding (cf. 7:1; 8:1) to a variety of questions about the nature and use of food associated with the pagan religions and the believer's relationship to the social element of the pagan temples. Whatever the details of the context, issues of knowledge (8:1, 4, 7, 10) and conscience (8:7, 10; 10:25, 27–29) were central to the problem. The delineation of persons as "weak" or "strong" relates to whether their worldview about idols was biblical or still tainted with paganism. One's worldview about idols determined how to view meat that was associated with the temple. The weak believers could not isolate the meat from association with their pagan background and therefore felt guilty if they ate it (8:7–8). The weak had weak consciences (8:7, 10) because their knowledge base was flawed, and therefore the pain caused by their conscience was wrong and misleading. The so-called strong believers had a correct worldview but lacked the grace to restrict their freedom for the good of their brethren (8:9–13). In this context, an action that is not a sin becomes a sin because of a relational violation in the believing community.

On the other hand, the question is often asked, "How long do you accommodate the weak?" Paul speaks plainly in the Corinthian context. To call someone "weak" in a public manner would not be a compliment. By so doing, Paul does not compromise the truth but extends grace to those who are in need of education in Christ. Paul calls for patience. At the same time, I think Paul would say that we tolerate inadequate knowledge until the weak have had a reasonable time to educate themselves and address their worldviews. If they refuse to do so, they move from the category of weakness to belligerence. Paul certainly did not hold back in naming these persons weak, a label no one would relish. At the same time, he identified with them in order to move them to a higher understanding (1 Cor. 9:22). Does this mean that Paul compromised a correct theology to accommodate the weak? No. He dealt with the situation in the open with a letter of public record and spoke the truth in love.

Let me illustrate this from my own experience. I was not raised in a Christian home, although my parents instilled in me the values of a Judeo-Christian upbringing. I was a rebellious teenager who would skip school and hang out at the local pool hall. In my town, a pool hall was a place to drink and gamble. Dedicated sinners, not saints, populated that pool hall. A few years later, while in the navy, I became a Christian. Caring believers directed me to seek out a Servicemen's Christian Center at my new duty station so that I might study the Bible and grow in Christian understanding. I remember the day I located my first center in New London, Connecticut. As I was halfway up the stairs to the center, I heard the familiar sound of billiard balls. I thought to myself, "I must be in the wrong place." I went back down the stairs and checked the sign. I had the right place. I went back up into the center and saw Christians playing a game I associated with that sinful pool hall back home. I was appalled. Slowly I learned that it was not the pool table but its location that made the difference. A good while later, after my knowledge base was adjusted, I was able to play pool and not feel guilty. The function of conscience always lags behind, because a change of view takes time. Conscience is a servant of our knowledge base, and when our knowledge has changed to the level of new convictions, conscience accommodates that change.

Paul's use of conscience in 1 Corinthians 10 is quite unique to the historical context. Paul instructs the believers to eat the meat from the market or a person's home without regard for conscience. The key phrase in the King James Version is "asking no question for conscience sake," translated "without raising questions of conscience" by the New International Version (10:25, 27). Some, hearing the King James rendering, have assumed that Paul suggested, "What you don't know won't hurt you!" Can you really imagine Paul giving that kind of advice? I don't think so. So what was he saying? Most likely, Paul took a slogan, "on account of conscience," used by the weak to manipulate those who would buy such meat and turned it back on them. There was no reason to ask questions of conscience, since a person with knowledge knew that the meat was not tainted because idols are nothing.

We have observed from the uses of the term in the New Testament that the conscience is a monitor of actions on the basis of the worldview and values we practice. Conscience does not communicate new information to us but merely stimulates us to maintain what we already know. Let's probe the role of conscience a bit more from the perspective of God's will and godly discernment.

Kinds of Values and Conscience

Our conscience reminds us of the values we recognize and apply. Values refer to the personal beliefs we hold about every area of life, from whether there is a God to which grocery store gives the best deals. It is helpful at this point to remind ourselves about the various categories of values. First, there are obligatory moral values—the clear commands of the Bible. No one who holds Christian values disputes this category. Second, there are community values—the beliefs and traditions of a given group of believers with which we associate ourselves. These values may not all be obligatory, but they do dictate participation in good standing with a community. For example, the consumption of wine at a meal is biblically permissible, but many modern Christian communities forbid the practice. In this case, one might forego a freedom for the benefit of the community. Third, there are personal values—the beliefs we all develop that make us who we are as individuals. For example, each of us values different kinds of music, food, exercise, hobbies, careers, and what we are free to do on Sunday.

The conscience monitors all levels of values equally. We will feel convicted in the same way, more or less, whether we violate a clear command not to lie, publicly violate a community standard, or violate our own personal standards. This is the job of the conscience. It does not discriminate the level of values; it merely monitors and holds us accountable to the ones we recognize and apply.

In our decision making, therefore, we must delineate the kind of value that we are dealing with when we feel the pressure of conviction. Knowing ourselves and why we think the way we do, we raise the conversations we have with ourselves to new levels.

Conscience and Godly Discernment

Conscience is a God-created function that monitors our beliefs within our self-reflective capacity as human beings. This aspect of our self-awareness produces pain and conviction when we violate our worldview and values. This function provides moral restraint for all human beings in reference to their values, whether Jew or Gentile, Christian or Muslim, religionist or atheist. While the values sets may differ, the function is the same. Conscience does not create values but merely monitors them as we have the moral-and-value-judgment conversations with ourselves. An external voice of God or the devil does not invade our space. Rather, that little voice is "ourselves talking to ourselves."

In light of the role of conscience, let me return to the dictum "Let your conscience be your guide." Should we follow this dictum? The answer is yes and no. Conscience is a guide in the sense that it convicts us to maintain our beliefs as we make decisions. This is why God created us with a conscience. Ignoring it creates moral/value chaos. On the other hand, conscience is not the final authority; it is dependent upon our beliefs and values. Therefore, the ultimate guidance system of our lives is our values set. If our values are wrong, conscience can do nothing but go along with them. Paul had a clear conscience about killing Christians until his own conversion. He thought he was serving God. Conscience is subject to critique in terms of the evaluation of the correctness of our worldview and values.

This brings us back to Romans 12 and the need for a transformed mind. Remember, the renewal of our minds is a restructuring of our beliefs and values systems—a constant and lifetime project. Transformation will not be complete until we are with Christ in eternity. If the transformed mind process restructures our values systems, we will experience internal tensions with the conscience—just like the weak in 1 Corinthians and myself with billiards. The final authority for right or wrong, as well as the continuum of godly discernment, comes from properly established and verified values. Conscience will eventually align itself with this educational process.

These reflections should help us see that Christians cannot make feelings and the little voices we hear the foundation for discerning life's decisions. Godly discernment is driven by a careful delineation of values.

The Feeling of Peace—Is It a Reason to Act or a Product of Doing Right?

During my years of teaching college students, I often had the privilege of talking with young couples about to be engaged. My first question to them was "Why do you think you should get married?" The usual answer was "Because we are so much in love." I would respond, "Why?" They would look at me oddly, wanting to say, "Where have you been?

Have you not seen how much in love we are?" They would often continue to respond with superficial reasons. I would continue to press and would eventually receive the answer, "Because God has given us such peace about our decision to marry." This answer was supposed to stop my persistent questions. In their minds, the answer presented two irrefutable reasons: God and our inner feelings, which, of course, are from God. Peace became the ultimate reason for action. What is the role of peace in will-of-God discernment?

The word *peace* occurs over ninety times in the New Testament. Its most frequent usage is for a translation of its Hebrew counterpart *shalom*. *Shalom* was more than a greeting. It conveyed a comprehensive wish for the well-being of the subject being greeted. Jesus used it to symbolize apostolic blessing (Matt. 10:13). It stilled the hearts of his troubled disciples in the postresurrection appearances (Luke 24:36; John 20:19, 21, 26). The term *peace* was linked with grace as the greeting in the salutary opening of the Epistles (Rom. 1:7; 1 Cor. 1:3; 2 Cor. 1:2; Gal. 1:3; Phil. 1:2; Col. 1:2; 1 Thess. 1:2; 2 Thess. 1:2; 1 Tim. 1:2; 2 Tim. 1:2; Titus 1:4; Philem. 3; 1 Peter 1:2; 2 Peter 1:2; 2 John 3; 3 John 14; Jude 2; Rev. 1:4).

Peace also represents a continuum of meaning in relation to conflict. It can relate to the absence of external conflict, a state of peace (Acts 9:31). It can depict the cessation of physical hostility (Matt. 5:9; 1 Cor. 7:15) or one's internal hostility toward God or others (Luke 2:14; John 16:33; Rom. 5:1). Peace can represent our reconciliation to God (Acts 10:36; Eph. 2:14–17; Col. 1:20; 2 Peter 3:14) or to others (Phil. 4:7). Conformity to God's moral will in the process of sanctification brings peace (Rom. 8:6).

Peace addresses a wide variety of experience, but it is never used scripturally as an internal barometer for gauging God's will. While Christians freely use the phrase "I know this is God's will because I have peace about it," the Bible never uses the term in this manner. Peace is a product of doing right, not a reason for action. This kind of an expression is similar to saying, "My conscience doesn't bother me, and therefore it must be okay." Conscience and peace are appealed to as evidence for action. If, as we have observed, this is an incorrect use of conscience, it is also an invalid use of peace. We have a clear conscience or we feel peace when we are not violating our values. We can, however, have these feelings and still be wrong if our values are incorrect.

Peace is never a reason to do something. Peace is a product, a feeling that comes when we are contemplating or acting in conjunction with the norms and values that we recognize and apply. Our values should be correct lest we have a false sense of peace. We are not to seek a sense of peace in order to act; we are to determine if an action is right and appropriate so that we can have a sense of peace. Peace does not justify actions; values do.

Consider the account of Euodia and Syntyche in Philippians 4. These two ladies were valuable workers in the early church. Their relationship, however, went sour. This breakdown was causing tension in the congregation. They were earning the nicknames "Odor" and "Stinky." Paul publicly appealed to them and the church to get their act together. He affirmed their value and pointed out the products that would be theirs once the problem was addressed (4:2–7). The familiar passage, "And the peace of God, which transcends all understanding, will guard your hearts and your minds in Christ Jesus" (4:7), promised the end result for the Philippian church once harmony was restored.

Conclusion

Conscience is a God-created function of our self-awareness that keeps us in touch with the norms and values we recognize and apply. It is a slave to our worldview and values set. Consequently, our task is to pursue a transformed mind in order to assure that the worldview and values that guide our lives are correct and appropriate.

Conscience relates to knowing God's will, because it monitors the revealed moral will of God and the structures of Christian worldview that we have developed. Conscience is not an independent voice in our soul as if it were outside of us speaking to us. It is the voice of our inner beings as we carry on this conversation of discernment within our minds. When data comes to us (see figure 5 on page 47), we immediately process it against our worldview and values. This "grid" interprets the data and renders an opinion about how it relates to us. If we are called upon to lie, our grid should remind us that lying violates God's moral law. We are convicted not to lie but tell the truth. This sets our course of action. If we are asked to buy a nonessential item beyond our means, even though we want it badly, our values should evaluate this opportunity to purchase in light of our means, our financial obligations, and the needs of our families. When this evaluation is complete, hopefully, we exercise the self-discipline to handle our funds in a responsible rather than a selfish manner.

The Role of the Spirit in God's Will and Godly Discernment

■ We began this book with an overview of epistemology—the sources, nature, and validity of knowledge. How do we know what we know, and how do we know that what we claim to know is valid? We saw that the solution for the problem of knowing ultimate truth about God and his will comes in a revelatory form. Without God's revealing role, humanity cannot know ultimate truth. The Bible is clear that the Holy Spirit, the third person of the Trinity, fulfills a crucial role in this revealing activity. The Spirit's role in the promotion of the knowledge of God is focused in two ways: the production of Scripture and the application of Scripture. Theologians refer to the inward conviction of the Spirit's application of Scripture as "the witness of the Spirit." We need to know something about these categories before we can address the role of the Spirit in reference to our knowing God's will. The ultimate question is not whether the Spirit is involved in our lives, but how he does his work in our lives at this time in redemptive history.

The Holy Spirit and the Production of the Bible

We saw earlier that 1 Corinthians 2:6–16 presents the Spirit as the agent of revelation to the apostles. A group within the church rejected Paul's authority and the message of the cross. In 1 Corinthians 1–4, Paul argued that his message was valid because it was not his own idea but one that God revealed. Chapter 2, verses 6–16, is at the center of this argument. The epistemological dilemma of 2:6–9 is solved in 2:10, "but God has revealed it to us by his Spirit." Therefore, the apostle's speech was the very word of God (cf. 14:37–38; 2 Peter 3:15–16). It was the work of the Spirit to ensure that the revelation to the apostles was correctly transferred into the documents we call Scripture (1 Cor. 2:10–13).

Peter also speaks about the role of the Spirit in the process of bringing God's message to the world. The prophets, agents of God who spoke his message, were "carried along by the Holy Spirit" (2 Peter 1:21). The metaphor of being carried along is like a ship at sea in a storm that has lost its ability to go where it wants (Acts 27:15, 27, the term *driven* is the same as *carried*). The ship is the same, the crew is the same, the personalities of each remain, but it is now subject to a greater power. The apostles understood that the Holy Spirit was the agent to communicate what became Scripture (Acts 1:16; 4:25; 28:25). The Bible does not explain how the Spirit accomplishes the transfer of God's mind to a human agent; it merely asserts it as true. Such contexts, however, are focused on special persons and are not open to application to just anyone. Texts of this type are often misused. John 14–16 contains Jesus' address to the eleven disciples about his departure and their future. The statement in John 16:13 that the Spirit "will guide you into all truth," is not a general promise to any Christian but is addressed to the disciples who would chronicle Jesus' earthly ministry and God's will for the church.

God's speech through prophets and apostles is unique. Much of what they communicated was eventually codified into what we call Scripture. Biblical texts that reflect this process cannot be applied to God's speaking to the typical believer. To do so violates the rule of contextual intent.

The Holy Spirit and the Application of Scripture: The Witness of the Spirit

The theology of the witness of the Spirit addresses three major areas where the Spirit convicts persons of the truth and validity of God's message. The function of the Spirit in the presentation of the triune godhead is to be the executor of God's will. The Spirit does not originate the divine plan but he accomplishes it in the flow of redemptive history. The Spirit testifies to things other than himself. He brings focus to the objects of redemptive proclamation. It is particularly the Spirit's role to bear witness to Christ, to the reality of salvation, and to the Word of God, the Scriptures.

During Jesus' earthly life, he appealed to the external witness of John the Baptizer, Jesus' own works, God the Father, and the Scriptures as validation of the truth of who he was (John 5:31–40). On the night before his death, Jesus talked at length with his disciples about what it would be like when he was gone (John 13–17). He detailed aspects of the Spirit's ministry to the apostles once he was gone.

He shifted to the Spirit as the one who would testify about him (John 15:26; Acts 5:32; 1 John 4:2) and glorify Jesus by focusing attention on the Son of God (John 16:14). The Spirit's testimony to the apostles relates to Jesus' earthly life and teaching and is eventually contained in the Gospels in our Bible. There is also a shift from an external to an internal witness. This is in keeping with the role of the Spirit to witness to something rather than originate new material in regard to Jesus. Believers today are now responsible to testify about Jesus from the content the apostles passed on to us. This kind of pattern continued in the early church and is reflected by Paul's comments in 1 Corinthians 15:1–8 and in 2 Timothy 2:2 where he charges his protégés to pass on the same teaching he had given in public.

Even more elaborate than the Spirit's witness to Christ is his internal testimony concerning the application of salvation. The Spirit convicts "the world of guilt in regard to sin and righteousness and judgment" (John 16:8). This conviction of sinners' internal processes must be in reference to a benchmark. The benchmark is the external gospel proclamation that the Spirit uses to do the internal work of conviction. After one has believed the proclamation and moved into the category of saved, the Spirit bears an internal witness to the reality of that transaction. Consider the following biblical statements.

> The Spirit himself testifies with our spirit that we are God's children.
>
> Romans 8:16

> And it is the Spirit who testifies, because the Spirit is the truth. . . . Anyone who believes in the Son of God has this testimony in his heart.
>
> 1 John 5:6, 10

True believers have a settled conviction within themselves that they know God (1 John 4:13; Gal. 4:6). This conviction is an evidence of the Spirit's work in salvation and assurance. However, this does not occur in a vacuum. The contexts of Romans and 1 John both focus on how the sanctifying process of obedience to truth confirms the reality of inward change. The Spirit works within this context to confirm in the believer the reality of that change.

The third aspect of the witness of the Spirit relates to the relationship of the Holy Spirit to the Word of God, the Bible. From 1 Corinthians 2:6–16 we found that the Spirit is a major player in the conveyance of God's mind through human instruments into the product of Scripture. This is a special work. We enjoy the benefits of the product but are not part of an ongoing process of revelation.

In addition to the process of revelation, the witness of the Spirit picks up where revelation ends and continues a work in reference to the Bible. The Spirit's role with the believer in relation to the Bible has often been popularly called "illumination." This term is not in the Bible and may be a poor choice because of the baggage that the average Christian may import into it. I have heard Christians equate illumination to revelation, that is, an extrabiblical process of direct communication from God to us. This is a flawed understanding. The work of the Spirit in the believer in relation to the Word is a work of conviction, not the communication of new content. It is a witness to the Word, not the conveyance of information in addition to the Word. The Spirit persuades us that the Word is true, authoritative, and worthy of obedience.

Illumination is often confused with revelation, even in the writings of theologians. Texts such as John 13–16, 1 Corinthians 2:6–16, and statements in the Gospels and Acts (Luke 12:12; Acts 11:28; 21:11) describe God's revelatory activity, not a process of illumination. These particular accounts are also unique within the flow of redemptive history. To equate the statements in these texts with the idea of illumination is to confuse the categories and create false expectations on the part of the current Christian community.

John's imagery of the anointing of the Spirit in his first Epistle illustrates this witness of the Spirit to truth proclaimed. John wrote to a community of believers that he had mentored. They were in jeopardy of moving away from what they had been previously taught to persuasive false teaching John calls "antichrists" (1 John 2:18–27). He reminded them of their "anointing from the Holy One" (2: 20, 27). This anointing accounts for why they know truth as truth (2:20–21). This truth that they had heard from the beginning of their contact with Christian teaching (2:24) was affirmed by the anointing, to which John refers as the indwelling Spirit of God.[1] Now consider 1 John 2:26–27:

> I am writing these things to you about those who are trying to lead you astray. As for you, the anointing you received from him remains in you, and you do not need anyone to teach you. But as his anointing teaches you about all things and as that anointing is real, not counterfeit—just as it has taught you, remain in him.

Have you ever had people tell you that you do not need to study or go to school to learn the Bible, because the indwelling Spirit is the only teacher you will ever need? Perhaps they quoted, "you do not need anyone to teach you" from this passage as a proof text for their assertion. If this is what John meant, then why did he bother writing? Why did Jesus give the Great Commission to "go and teach"? Why did Paul tell his followers to teach others? Why are teaching and teachers' gifts given to the church?

Obviously, this passage does not mean that we do not need teachers. The insertion of one word in John's statement can bring out the meaning in context, "you do not need anyone *else* to teach you." John was merely reminding his disciples that, because the Spirit had confirmed what they had been taught from the beginning as true, they did not now need to listen to the false teachers.

What is the Holy Spirit's role in our acquisition of knowledge of God? His role is to convict us that biblical teaching is true, authoritative, and worthy of our obedience. The Spirit and the Word are not in competition. The Spirit bears witness to the Word and holds us to it. The Spirit's work causes our "inner eyes" to see, to really see. This sight is the kind that engages truth until it changes us. This is Paul's prayer in Colossians 1 and Ephesians 1. The mystery had been revealed to the apostles and prophets throughout redemptive history (Eph. 3:2–6). Now the Spirit works within believers to enable us to engage what has been revealed in order to know better both God and his teachings (Eph. 1:17–18). How this internal work is performed is not explained, it is merely asserted as a fact. This internal work of the Spirit, however, is not a work of new revelation but one that helps us engage what God has already revealed and makes that truth the center of our worldview and values set. It is a work of persuasion in relation to the Word. This is all part of the mandate of Romans 12, "Be transformed by the renewing of your mind."

The Spirit and Guidance: What Do "Led" and "Filled" Mean?

Certain passages in the New Testament present the same question we reviewed in our discussion of guidance examples in the Old Testament: What is normative? A number of texts reflect direct supernatural guidance by the Spirit in the New Testament. Accounts of God's activity with Philip (Acts 8), Peter (Acts 10–11), and Paul (Acts 13:2; 16:6–7; 20:22–23) depict such guidance. Are these patterns, however, designed to be normative for Christians after the apostolic age? These texts particularly describe the foundational spread of the gospel during the apostolic age. Some have claimed that they are normative, but the evidence they present has little likeness to the original New Testament events. I view such examples as descriptive and nonnormative for the process of guidance in the postapostolic period.

What does all of this have to do with knowing God's will for your life? The Spirit's role in guidance is to do an internal work that correlates with God's Word rather than going beyond that Word with extrabiblical communication. If we do not absorb God's Word into our reasoning process, we rob the Spirit of what he needs to do his work of conviction and persuasion. One example of this is to consider the texts that tell us to be "led by the Spirit":

> Because those who are led by the Spirit of God are sons of God.
>
> Romans 8:14

> But if you are led by the Spirit, you are not under law.
>
> Galatians 5:18

Led in both passages is used as a metaphor of sanctification and does not represent extrabiblical Spirit guidance. The Spirit's guidance in these contexts is to convict and compel us to live godly as biblical teaching directs. Romans and Galatians are both contexts dealing with the process of sanctification in the believer.[2] Sanctification is a status and a process. Those who believe in Jesus have been sanctified, "set apart," as the redeemed. The redeemed must also pursue holiness (Heb. 12:14; Eph. 1:4; Phil. 3:12; 1 Thess. 4:3–4). This pursuit is part of our being morally transformed into the image of Christ (1 Cor. 13:12; 1 John 3:1–3). In addition to the metaphor "led," Paul also uses the metaphor of "walk" in the Spirit (Gal. 5:16; Eph. 4:1; "walk" is translated as "live" in modern versions). The phrase "led by the Spirit" has particularly been lifted from its context and claimed as a direct voice of the Spirit to each believer as a part of guidance. This is often extended to account for the inner voices that we experience. Such proposals, however, miss the contexts of Romans and Galatians.

Romans 6–8 are classic chapters on the concepts of positional and progressive sanctification. Sanctification is the biblical teaching about our legal standing before God (positional) and our responsibility to grow in our obedience to God's teaching (progressive). Paul rehearses his own life's experience in knowing God and dealing with sin. Chapter 7 is the "do be do be do" chapter! Paul says,

> I do not understand what I do. For what I want to do I do not do, but what I hate I do. And if I do what I do not want to do, I agree that the law is good. . . . For what I do is not the good I want to do; no, the evil I do not want to do—this I keep on doing. Now if I do what I do not want to do, it is no longer I who do it, but it is sin living in me that does it.
>
> Romans 7:15–20

In Romans 6–8, Paul addresses the moral battle between the flesh and the spirit. As Christians, we know what is right but we lack the power to do it. Knowing right is not the problem, doing it is. Right is known from the truth God has revealed. Paul's answer to this moral dilemma of our will is that the indwelling Spirit of God enables us to "put to death the misdeeds of the body" (8:13) so that we might live God's way. When we do this, our moral behavior evidences the work of the Spirit in our lives and, therefore, proves to the world and us that we are "sons of God." Paul's metaphor, "led by the Spirit," merely asserts that this moral victory is the result of God's Spirit enabling the believer to live as God has directed in his Word. This is the Spirit's work of convicting the believer to live in accordance with the Word. Consequently, in Romans 8:14, Paul uses religious language to state that when we live by God's truth we demonstrate that we are God's children. God's Spirit is the one who makes this life possible, because he enables us through being born again (regeneration) to obey God's Word. Paul uses the term *led* as a metaphor to affirm the Spirit's work in accordance with God's teaching. This is analogous to 1 Corinthians 12:3, where Paul states, "no one can say, 'Jesus is Lord,' except by the Holy Spirit." Obviously, any person can utter the words "Jesus is Lord." But to submit to Jesus as Lord, the essence of recognizing that he is Lord, is a work of the convicting Spirit.

Galatians 5:18 also speaks of sanctification. The context of Galatians 5–6 is sort of like a sandwich (see figure 10 on page 131). The pieces of bread are 5:13–15 and 6:1–13, setting the boundaries of the context. Galatians 5:14, "The entire law is summed up in a single command: 'Love your neighbor as yourself,'" is balanced with 6:2, "Carry each other's burdens, and in this way you will fulfill the law of Christ." Then 5:16–26 is the contents of the sandwich, offering an exposition of what it means to love your neighbor. The works of the flesh are evidence that one does not love his neighbor (5:19–21) and the fruit of the Spirit is an exposition of what it means to love your neighbor (5:22–26). When the believing community demonstrates the characteristics listed as the fruit of the Spirit, they show that they are "led by the Spirit" (5:18). The Spirit convicts and energizes the community to live in conformity to divine standards in attitudes and actions. When we do, we show that we are truly God's children.

Fulfill God's Law: Love your neighbor as yourself (Galatians 5:13–15).

Exposition of hating and loving your neighbor . . . works
of the flesh and fruit of the Spirit (Galatians 5:16–21; 5:22–26)

Fulfill Christ's Law: Love your neighbor by bearing one another's burdens (Galatians 6:1–5).

Fig. 11. Galatians 5–6 in Context

Another Pauline metaphor is to be "filled" with the Spirit. In chapter 6, when we examined Colossians 1, we saw that the metaphor "filled" means to be "characterized." This same meaning also fits Ephesians 5:18, where "be filled with the Spirit," reflects one being characterized by godly behavior. The word *controlled* is often used to explain the "fill" metaphor, but it does not capture the meaning of the contexts where this use occurs. In Ephesians 5, "speaking" (v. 19), "giving thanks" (v. 20), and "submitting" (v. 21) actually modify the intransitive verb "fill" in 5:18, and thereby provide the key to its meaning. The phrase "with the Spirit," sets the environment of characterization rather than its content. A life characterized by the traits of Ephesians 5:19–21 is one lived in accordance with the Spirit's persuasion.

The Spirit is the divine agent of moral development. He correlates the Word of God with our reflections in order to convict us to apply our worldview and values set. When the believer demonstrates the moral truth the Bible teaches, she is "led" by the Spirit. This work of the Spirit is never apart from the Bible but in consort with it. The Spirit's internal work is like that of the conscience. It is a work of conviction in reference to something. It is impossible to delineate these internal works into clean packages of definition. The subjective domain is real, but it requires the objective Word, our alignment with that Word, and God's sovereign care to interpret the subjective domain.

To claim that "led by the Spirit" or "filled with the Spirit" implies some mystical connection whereby extrabiblical information is conveyed for the purpose of guidance is to violate the contexts where these statements occur. Paul's use of metaphors to frame religious language is open to abuse by those who read his writings. Figures of speech must be explained. The integrity of a literary context should protect such speech and its explanation. When these contexts are violated, however, a reader's imagination is his only limitation.

The Gifting of Believers and God's Will

Paul describes the presence of spiritual giftedness in the church as a work of the Spirit (1 Corinthians 12). How does the Spirit's work in gifting relate to our knowing God's will for our lives? The simple answer is that God expects us to serve in the church by the exercise of our giftedness as recognized by the church. We do not tell the church what our gifts are, the church tells us. Gifts emerge and are recognized as such in the midst of service. Each of us fulfills a contribution to God's kingdom expressed in the church by this service. This is part of God's declared will. Just do it.

The exercise of gifts is a "manifestation[s] of the Spirit" (1 Cor. 12:7) in the sense that our gifts reflect the presence of God in the congregation empowered by the Spirit. In the early church, there were miraculous manifestations. Study 1 Corinthians 12:8–11, where the entire list represents miracle-type gifts. The list is crafted with eight items, "miraculous powers" being the hinge in the middle, giving context to the others. The eight items may well be four doubles: message of wisdom/knowledge, faith/healing—miraculous powers—prophecy/discerning of spirits (not demons but the spirits of prophets), tongues/interpretation of tongues.[3]

The standard Greek term for "gift" never occurs as a label for these expressions in the Greek Bible. English has used *gift* to translate the Greek words *charisma* (a bestowment of divine grace in biblical literature, other forms can be construed as a "gracious gift") and *pneumatikos* (the adjective for "spiritual"). We have sometimes read a popularized "Christmas" idea into the term gift and thereby may misconstrue the nature of these functions within the church. The nonmiraculous spiritual gifts cited by Paul are not special endowments that we never had before conversion. Rather, they are the development of our innate talents within the context of the believing community and its activities.

The Bible contains only four lists of these manifestations that we call gifts (Rom. 12:6–8; 1 Cor. 12:8–10; 12:28; Eph. 4:11; cf. 1 Peter 4:7–11). The lists are varied and each serves a different purpose in context. We should remember that any given list is never complete and that all lists combined do not represent everything that could be included. Lists are representative. The gift lists we have contain items ranging from something requiring a miracle to the gift of helping. It seems best to understand the nonmiraculous gifts as the emergence in the congregation of persons who are skilled in certain ways. Some can teach, some cannot. Some are encouragers, some are not. Some are leaders, some are not. Some are "gifted" at showing mercy or giving to others, some are not. These gifts, and all that we might add to the list in our culture, should not be read as requiring a miraculous bestowment of something we did not possess prior to conversion. Gifts are spiritual gifts because we now fulfill our natural giftedness under the umbrella of the church rather than the world. In this sense, the gifts are spiritual and credited to the Spirit who superintends the church.

Conversion brings out our true natures and takes us to the level we are capable of achieving. I well remember how unfocused I was as an unsaved young adult. I was shy. I did not like to read. School was not my thing. Conversion brought me out. Now I speak to large audiences regularly. My vocation is reading and teaching. I possessed these skills prior to conversion, but I was not living in a context to exercise my gifts. The church gave me that context and encouraged me along. The Spirit of God moved me in ways that can never be explained to fulfill my "destiny." God's providence set the stage in unexplainable ways.

Spiritual gifts, therefore, are part of God's will for our lives. We do not "find" our role through some mystical process. We do not wait till we "find" what we should do in order to serve God in the church. We get involved and in so doing, God's plan is fulfilled in amazing ways.

Conclusion

The Holy Spirit is intimately involved in the fulfillment of God's will in the world and in our lives. The question for us is how does the Spirit's work evidence itself in this process? The Bible records many miraculous aspects of the Spirit's direct intervention into redemptive history and in bringing the written Bible into being. But is this our model for the Spirit's normative role in the guidance of individual believers today? Perhaps reflecting upon our conversion experience will help us to image how the Spirit works in our lives today. I will use my own story as an illustration.

As I mentioned earlier, I was not raised in a Christian home. I never saw my dad in a church. I had only modest contact with any church while growing up, and that contact was more for Boy Scouts than Awana! I was a rebellious teenager and joined the navy at seventeen. When I arrived at boot camp, the Gideons distributed pocket New Testaments. I tried to read mine but could not understand what I was reading. At the time, I did not even associate Jesus' birthday with Christmas. At the same time, in retrospect, I was in the process of conviction by the Spirit of my need to know God. It felt like an internal uneasiness and a thirst for a religious experience that I could not explain. There were no voices, just a "pressure" to look into things Christian. Yet I avoided preaching like a plague. While at home on leave, I "happened" into a Vacation Bible School setting where kids were dressed up like Indians and the teacher was telling the story of the prodigal son. I figured it would not hurt me to listen since this was not church! The telling of that parable began to give me a new understanding of God and myself. An old friend of the family took me to church a week or so later. My memory of the service is a blur, but I still remember vividly the invitation at the end of the sermon. I was very uncomfortable (i.e., under conviction). I did not want to get mixed up with a Christian commitment. But when the preacher asked us to bow our heads and close our eyes, something strange happened. I saw the light! Well, sort of. When you close your eyes in an emotional state you have a sort of white light flash in the process. Previously, I had persecuted Christians verbally with the mocking song "I Saw the Light." But when that natural phenomenon of closing my eyes caused a flash of light, it hit me like a rock concert floodlight. I did not know ten cents about Christian truth, but I had the superstition that if "you see the light" and reject it, you are toast! That event moved me to respond to the invitation, have someone explain salvation to me, and respond in a simple prayer for salvation. I was thoroughly "saved" that day. The Spirit used even my superstitious view of "light" to move me into a context where the truth of salvation through the work of Christ could be explained. My journey since that moment confirms that I responded appropriately to the Spirit's conviction.

Now, was that "light" a miracle? No. Did I hear audible voices? No. I certainly had an internal conversation with myself, but was that God's audible voice speaking? No. Rather, the meshing of events, a modest knowledge, and the unexplainable internal conviction of the Spirit brought it all together to cause my conversion.

What about my Christian journey up to now, some forty years after this event? How has the Spirit accomplished God's will in my life? How has he led me in a walk that results in the moral development that the Bible demands? How did he lead me from the navy, through school, and into vocational Christian teaching? He did it in the same way, with an unexplainable internal conviction that drove me to the Word and service every day. It has been quite a trip.

Conviction is the work of the Spirit in guidance. Our work is to determine the right or wrong of what we are convicted about in terms of our biblical worldview and values set. We are responsible to pursue godly discernment in this matrix. We can rest in the fact that God will fulfill his will in this process.

The Bible does not present a model of the indwelling Spirit providing secret access to the mind of God as a norm to discern the will of God. There is no special category of enlightened Christians who have unique access to the mind of God. We all have equal opportunity to know God's will by being a "workman who does not need to be ashamed and who correctly handles the word of truth" (2 Tim. 2:15).

It is not the role of the Spirit to provide ongoing communication of God's will to us. Neither is the Spirit's work to reveal the future to believers on request. The Spirit's role for the Christian is that of conviction and persuasion in reference to God's Word. This conviction is not limited to a particular text, no more than the development of our worldview and values is. The Spirit's work relates to the whole process of the transformed mind. The problem is that we do not have a means to detect when an internal conviction is from conscience, the Spirit, or our own desires. That is why we need an objective procedure to make decisions that are based on the validation of our understanding of the Bible and the worldview and values set we claim. This is not as comfortable or as safe as having a direct revelatory process, but it is a process that God has designed to develop us as persons created in his image.

We have observed that the conscience and the Spirit play similar roles, both performing the task of internal conviction. The conscience convicts us about the values that we recognize and apply. The Spirit convicts us about what Scripture teaches and the values we derive from it. It is impossible to know whether our internal sense of conviction comes from conscience or Spirit in most cases. The key issue is that we have to test all our feelings of conviction by an objective analysis of the Bible's teaching and our own application of its values. If an internal sense of conviction contradicts the Scriptures, we can be assured that it is not a conviction of the Spirit. If our feeling of conviction is in concord with the Bible and our values, then we must respond.

Prayer and God's Will — 10

■ Pastor Tom was working on his next Sunday sermon when Dan burst into his office. "Pastor," he said, "I need you to pray for me." Dan was the Sunday school superintendent for the church, married to Joan, and the father of three rambunctious boys.

"What do you want me to pray about, Dan?"

"Well, I just got this phone call from my boss with a wonderful offer to advance within my company. Joan and I have talked about it but we cannot find peace about what to do and we need prayer. I really want to know God's will in this decision. Will you pray that God will show me what to do?"

"Tell me more," said Pastor Tom.

Dan reviewed his current employment. He worked out of a home office on his computer and traveled two or three days a month to visit clients. He was a middle manager making very good money. Joan also had a career as a nurse.

Dan's home-based setting allowed them the flexibility they needed to care for three young boys without daycare or the boys leaving or returning home without a parent present. The new position in the company would change Dan's life drastically. He would begin to travel fifteen days or so a month, with some extended international trips. He would be gone over a weekend each month and sometimes, but rarely, two weekends. He would have to move his office to the regional headquarters because he would supervise other persons.

Dan and Joan were focused on the salary increase Dan would receive—nearly fifty percent more. He would break into six figures for the first time! This extra money would help them achieve their college fund goals for the boys as well as their eventual retirement. Joan might even be able to reduce her hours to alleviate some care issues with the boys.

Dan explained to Pastor Tom that he did not have to take this offer to be secure within the company, but he was impressed that this was coming so early in his career. Surely the very fact of an offer might indicate God's will. Pastor Tom listened intently as Dan explained the situation. The greater the detail, the more obvious the value conflicts became. As Dan rehearsed the scenario out loud, he began to become aware of these conflicts and rationalize how to deal with his family versus career values. At one point he commented to Pastor Tom, "I don't think it is how much time I spend with the boys and Joan, but how I spend the time I do. Didn't you once observe that in one of your sermons?" Dan was beginning to feel the value tension as he thought out loud with his pastor, but he and Joan were so overwhelmed with the opportunity, they lacked objectivity in their analysis.

After listening for some time, Pastor Tom said, "Dan, have you and Joan written out a chart of the issues and values involved in this decision like I explained in my recent series on God's will?"

"Well, we did a little bit of that," Dan replied.

"What did you learn about the decision by that process, Dan?"

Dan chuckled nervously and said, "We thought you might ask that question!" Pastor Tom laughed and helped to relieve a bit of the tension. "But Pastor," Dan inquired, "Why are we so often caught between conflicting values? Why can't we find a way to have our cake and eat it too?"

"Sometimes you can," Pastor Tom replied, "but the values that relate to each decision will vary greatly. If the boys were in college or married, your chart would take on a very different structure. So Dan," Pastor Tom continued, "how do you think we should pray about this?"

"Well, Pastor," Dan replied, "I know what my values are telling me to do, I'm just a little slow in listening. I guess I need for you to pray that Joan and I will have the courage to do what we really believe is right for this time in our lives."

"That's worth praying for," replied Pastor Tom as he bowed his head.

Prayer Is Subject to God's Will

Variations of this scenario confront Christian families constantly. Skilled and hardworking persons always have more opportunities than they can fulfill. Every decision we confront is filled with value conflict. Sometimes it is a clear conflict of right and wrong, sometimes it is the difference between good, better, and best. Prayer is not a divining rod to settle the decision. We need the guidance of biblical values in order to deal with life's circumstances. We need to know what values drive us in order to pray appropriately.

Our knowledge of God is foundational to our worldview and our understanding of prayer. God is all-powerful, good, and loving. Yet he does not always exercise his power to accomplish the good things we pray about. For example, how many of us have prayed for the salvation of a loved one only to watch him seemingly die in unbelief? How many have prayed for a wayward child only to watch her destroy herself? We wonder, where is this good and all-powerful God who claims to love us? Or perhaps we become depressed because we assume that something is wrong in us that hindered God from responding to our petitions. This kind of thinking does not adequately account for prayer and God's will.

Does God answer prayer? Yes. The Bible says, "Ask and it will be given to you" (Matt. 7:7–8). But is this an unconditional promise so that we always get whatever we request? No. Neither are our faith and personal godliness the ultimate keys to having our prayers answered. Godly people often find their prayers unanswered. Unanswered prayer is not a barometer of spirituality. Jesus' prayer in Gethsemane illustrates that the sovereign will of God is the ultimate arbitrator of answered prayer. The "cup" with which Jesus struggled (Matt. 26:36–46; Luke 22:39–46) probably refers to that period on the cross when he cried out, "My God, my God, why have you forsaken me?" (Matt. 27:45–46; Mark 15:33–34). The honesty of Jesus' soul confesses that it was a cup he would choose to avoid. He prayed to avoid it. But instead, he yielded to the will and plan of God. Jesus' understanding of God's plan as revealed in the Scripture he studied, along with his unique relationship with the Father, shaped all of Jesus' prayers. Accepting

God's sovereign will in the outcome of our prayers is our greatest expression of faith. This kind of faith is the product of a worldview that is informed about who God is.

Consider John the Baptist. The families of John and Jesus were close. John was only six months older than Jesus (see Luke 1:23–26). During their childhood they probably saw each other twice a year during the spring and fall religious festivals in Jerusalem. When Jesus was missing once after the caravan returned north following a Passover festival, Mary and Joseph had assumed wrongly that Jesus was with some relative or friends (Luke 2:41–50). I think he and John spent lots of time together at festivals and the parents assumed they were together again. The conversations of John and Jesus must have been most interesting, especially since John never really knew that Jesus was the Messiah until after he baptized him (John 1: 29–34). John never called Jesus the Lamb of God until after the baptism event. The information of the birth narratives, which are so clear to us, was evidently so austere to these families, that they did not fully grasp its significance.

John did a fine job of being the forerunner to the Messiah. After Jesus' baptism, a quiet year of Jesus' ministry began as John transited out of attention (the "year of obscurity" is only recorded in John 1–4). John repeatedly points out Jesus as the Lamb of God, and John's disciples began to shift to Jesus (see John 1:35–42). This became the pattern, so much so that John's disciples eventually complained, "Everyone is going to him" (John 3:26; see also 4:1–3). John viewed all of this as part of his introduction of the Messiah saying, "He must become greater; I must become less" (John 3:30). Well into Jesus' first year of ministry, John was imprisoned (Luke 3:19–20).

Seeing the closeness of John and Jesus brings the account of John in prison in Luke 7:18–35 into clearer focus. While

John languished in Herod's prison, he began to wonder why he was missing the biggest event in Jewish history, especially since he was the vice-president of this event! I believe we can assume that John prayed much about his plight and the questions he had. When the opportunity presented itself, he sent his disciples to Jesus with the question, "Are you the one who was to come, or should we expect someone else" (Luke 7:19)? This odd question, in light of John 1–4, reflected John's discouragement and confusion. He was not seeking prominence, but if Jesus was the Messiah, John perhaps thought he should be involved. This question surely reflected an aspect of John's prayers in his prison seclusion. Jesus did not give a direct answer to John's disciples, but instead cited biblical texts and challenged John to draw his own conclusions (Luke 7:22–23). As soon as John's disciples departed to deliver Jesus' message, Jesus reflected to his audience on the greatness of John, calling him the greatest born among women (Luke 7:28). John probably died without hearing about Jesus' comments.

If the greatest person ever born experienced a silent heaven, then what right do we have to demand whatever we request of God? God answers prayer in accord with his will. While John's life ended in Herod's prison, it would be God's will to deliver Peter from a similar fate at a later time (Acts 12). God is not obligated to inform us when something is or is not his sovereign will. It is merely our obligation to pray and then accept the results as God's will.

Prayer Fulfills God's Will

If it is true that prayer is subject to God's sovereign plan and will, then why pray? The answer is simple. Because God has commanded us to pray, and in his own wisdom, he has designed that our prayers are a part of his plan. He has not chosen, however, to reveal his plan ahead of time. Therefore we often find our prayers, even good and appropriate prayers, to suffer mixed conclusions. God expects us to rest in his goodness and wisdom whatever the outcome of our prayers may be. Prayer does not form God's will but is an obedient response to God's expectations for us.

Prayer is a response to God's moral will. We are commanded to pray. In fact, the verbal forms of prayer language are usually in the imperative mood! "Our Father in heaven, . . . *give us* today our daily bread. *Forgive us* our debts . . . *lead us* . . . *deliver us* . . ." (Matt. 6:9–13, emphasis added). Prayer is not a bashful exercise. Yet I believe we all sense that it is not a bossing exercise either. Prayer requires that we balance the boldness God expects of us with a worldview that respects God's space and prerogatives. We pray for our burdens without reservations, but we accept the ultimate outcome of our prayers as God's will. We are the dependent creatures. Only God is independent. Prayer is a way of life, which demonstrates our dependence on God (1 Thess. 5:17). As Paul states it, "Be joyful always; pray continually; give thanks in all circumstances, for this is God's will for you in Christ Jesus" (1 Thess. 5:16–18).

When Paul exhorts us to "give thanks in all circumstances," he assumes that some circumstances are not positive. Paul expects us to engage the negative settings of life rather than look for a way out of them. Joy, prayer, and a thankful spirit in whatever settings we find ourselves are attitudes that reflect a life led by the Spirit to fulfill God's will.

Prayer Rests in God's Sovereign Will

Prayer recognizes God's sovereign will. In Jesus and John we saw examples of unanswered prayer in light of the greater purposes of God's plan. Jesus reflected his knowledge of these purposes, and although he struggled with what it meant in his life, he submitted himself to God's plan. John's struggle probably lasted to the end without the benefit of the same kind of insight. I would like to assume that when John received the report from his messengers conveying Jesus' quoting the Old Testament and point-ing out how those events are now fulfilled in his earthly ministry, John's previous confidence in Jesus as Messiah was renewed. Godly people demonstrate trust in spite of circumstances. Yet John may have died without hearing Jesus' statements.

The relationship of prayer to the fulfillment of God's plan has generated a great deal of discussion among theologians. Terrance Tiessen published a book entitled *Providence and Prayer: How Does God Work in the World?*[1] Tiessen details eleven major theological systems that address this question! Just a glance at this volume makes it clear that our view of prayer is a product of our larger theological understand-ing of who God is and how he carries out his work in the world.

I view prayer as instrumental, as part of the process that God has ordained to accomplish his purposes in the world. Our prayers are directly related to the fulfillment of God's will in the world. But prayer does not manipulate God's ultimate purposes. Rather God has designed his plan so that our prayers participate in the fulfillment of his eternally wise purposes. Because we do not know God's sovereign will ahead of time, answers to the way we pray are always conditioned by conformity to that will. This is the assumption behind the apostle John's statement "that if we ask anything according to his will, he hears us" (1 John 5:14). John is not exhorting us to find God's will but to condition our prayers to conform to it. This condition brings us back to our responsibility to discern God's desires from our transformed worldview. The better we know God and how he runs his world, the more likely we are to pray appropriately in the situations that confront us. But whatever the case, and whatever the outcome in our eyes, we must pray.

Prayer Is a Mature Response to Life's Circumstances

The Bible never exhorts us to pray to know God's will in advance in order to pray for its fulfillment. Prayer is not a means to gain knowledge of the future in order to conform prayer to that future. If this is so, then you might ask what the prayer in James 1:5–6 means: "If any of you lacks wisdom, he should ask God, who gives generously to all without finding fault, and it will be given to him." James's call to prayer is set in his teaching about our responses to life's trials. He exhorts us to endure (1:2–4), to pray (1:5–8), to accept the providential orderings of life (1:9–11), and to continue to endure (1:12). I find it informative that James does not give prayer as the first response to unexpected trials. Prayer is not our first line of defense when trials occur; our own spiritual maturity is our first response (the point of James 1:2–4). Prayer is second because it is a product of our maturity. This is once again a transformed-mind issue. If we are developing in our Christian worldview, prayer will come naturally and quickly when we encounter the difficulties of life, because prayer is an expression of our dependence on God.

James exhorts us to ask God for wisdom. It is not a request for knowledge. Wisdom in the Bible is a *product* of knowledge. This prayer for wisdom in the midst of a disaster is actually a prayer for God to help us process from our worldview why bad things happen to God's people.

Bringing our knowledge of God and his ways to bear on explaining the pain of life provides the wisdom we need to endure. For example, if a drunk driver kills a child, how do we respond? How do we deal with such a horrible event? Do we become angry with God for not preventing it? Do we piously dismiss the event by saying, "God has a purpose in this that we have to discover," and thereby deny the pain we feel without understanding why? The only way to respond to such human tragedy is to come to grips with our worldview. We need to wisely delineate how God has chosen to intervene or not intervene into life's events. For example, we need to incorporate into our worldview the fact that God did not choose to intervene for John the Baptist, the greatest man born of woman.

James's call to pray for wisdom is a call to process life's events in light of our biblical worldview. An informed believer understands that life's bad events do not mean that God does not love us. Rather, they remind us that we live in a messed up world, and God does not always choose to intervene for our safety or comfort. Godly believers today face death in many parts of our world. They pray for God's protection while they are brutally raped or murdered. Such actions against persons clearly violate God's moral will. Therefore, when we pray that God fulfill what we know his desires to be, why do we not have what we request? Because for reasons unknown to us, God has chosen not to intervene, and we must accept that reality without losing faith.

Conclusion

Prayer, in and of itself, fulfills God's will because we are commanded to pray. We should not hesitate to pray in light of our concerns and burdens. There are no limits as long as our prayers are within the boundaries of God's moral will. Yet we have all experienced mixed results in regard to our requests. These results indicate to us in hindsight God's sovereign will about the matters of our concerns. Sometimes it brings us joy and encouragement; sometimes it tests our faith. Our responsibility is to continue to obey God by praying while we also submit ourselves to the results that reflect a God who is wiser than us and whose purposes in the world are beyond our understanding.

Part 4

Reflections on God's Will Applied

This final section will provide you with sample reflections upon the process of thinking biblically and personally about a variety of life's decisions.

11

"Q & A" on Discerning God's Will

■ Pastor Don served in a small rural church and seldom saw anyone during the day. Most of his appointments were in the evening. He saw Judy pull into the parking lot through his window. She was one of the setup crew for summer vacation Bible school. His mind began to review Judy's life situation. She was married to George and they had three fine children. Judy and the kids were Christians and involved in church, but George was an unbeliever. He was a good provider, husband, and father. He even attended church functions with the family from time to time. Pastor Don had conversed with him about the gospel, but George quietly dismissed any need for Christian beliefs. In fact, George was so passive that it was difficult to stimulate him to think about eternity. George's passivity allowed Judy her space for church, but it also contributed to her "quiet desperation." They loved each other, but it was not the kind of love that addressed the deepest longings of Judy's soul. A couple of years back Judy had discussed with Pastor Don that years of prayer and being a good wife had not resulted in George's salvation. She was discouraged and angry that God had not answered her prayers. She wondered if it was God's will for her to remain married to an unbeliever.

Pastor Don reviewed the biblical teaching about marriage with Judy at that time. They saw that marriage was created by God and intended to be "till death do us part." They found no information that an "unequal yoke" marriage invalidated the marital union and expectations of longevity. Furthermore, George was sexually faithful to Judy and bent over backwards to be a good husband, and father, except for a Christian confession. As Judy reflected on these issues, she concluded that God's moral will required that she commit herself to George, endeavor to deepen their personal relationship, do all in her power to have a happy home, and continue to pray for her husband's salvation. Pastor Don continued to build a relationship with George and the family. He wished that some of his "Christian homes" were as solid as this one.

This chapter will pose a number of situations about which Christians ask, "What is God's will for . . . ?" After presenting a question, I will "think out loud" about how to answer it. Each of us must engage discernment about God's will in our own context. Different persons may address questions not directly answered by Scripture differently. There is no one answer for everyone about how we deal with singleness, adoption, models of parenting, educational choices, church selection, use of time and money, and many other issues. When the Bible clearly addresses an issue, we are all equally bound by what it says. But when we are developing answers to questions from a biblical worldview and values system because there is no one clear text, then we see diversity surface within the believing community. God, for his own purposes, planned life to work in this manner so that we might glorify him by the use of our created capacities. While believers may have differences, we will all answer to God for how we applied our worldview and values to life's issues.

Please remember the thesis of this book: Knowing God's will is not a process of receiving immediate information from God about life's issues but one of discerning life's issues on the basis of the revelation that God has already given to us. The Bible is the only accurate record of that revelation. God has not chosen for us to accomplish discernment by receiving immediate revelatory answers to our questions. Rather, he has given us his Word, and we are to deal with life from a biblical perspective. We must discern life's issues from the standpoint of biblical teaching and the worldview and values set we develop. Therefore, when we ask the question "What is God's will for _____?" we are required to ask, "What does the Bible teach about _____?" in order to begin to frame an answer for the question of God's will in that situation.

Please remember, much prayer should accompany all decisions. As I have stated previously, prayer is not a way of manipulating God but a way to bear our souls to God and submit to his sovereign wisdom. Prayer keeps us focused on God and our biblical values during the decision-making process. As the decision-making chart indicated (see figure 7 on page 65), all aspects of discernment are to be "carried out with an attitude of prayer for discerning wisdom and an attitude of submission to God's sovereign providence." When I do not repeat this fact in the following discussions, do not assume that it is not important. Please assume it is foundational to the process, and be sure to practice prayer in your analysis of decisions. At the same time, I would remind you that prayer is not a substitute for careful thinking about decisions. God has ordained that prayer and reason work together.

I have provided a sample list of life situation questions under several major categories representing some of the most influential aspects of our lives. The list was constructed by conversations with a variety of Christians and church groups. These include:

God's Will for Human Relationships

Whom should I marry?

What about having children? Adoption?

What about singleness?

What if I am married to an unbeliever?

What about divorce?

What if I am "single again"?

What about models of parenting?

What about those "Only Do Business with Christians" brochures?

What about cloistered Christian communities?

What about friendships with non-Christians?

What about my involvement in moral and political causes?

What about the care of aging parents?

God's Will for Career Decisions

How should I educate my children . . . home school, private, or public?

How do I choose a place for higher education?

What career should I pursue?

What about making career changes?

God's Will for Church Relationships

Where should I go to church?

What about making a church change?

What role should I play in my church?

What level of involvement should I accept?

God's Will for Life Stewardship

How can/should I use my time?

What about the use of my "leisure" time?

What about my money?

Should I plan for the future? Investments? Retirement?

God's Will for Special Issues

What about artificial insemination?

What about turning off "artificial life support"?

Should a Christian perform combat military service?

What about lawsuits?

What is a "call to ministry"?

How should a church view "the call of a pastor"?

At one time or another, most Christians have struggled with knowing God's will for these kinds of questions. If you have understood the model for knowing God's will that this book presents, you now know that the process to answer these questions is first to come to grips with the biblical teaching and worldview that applies to each, then to deal with how each item relates to the values that you have developed. We cannot treat all of these questions in our current setting. My purpose is to suggest how to think about these issues. I will reflect on representative questions from each category in order to illustrate the model presented in this book. No one can answer these questions for you, nor should they. You must learn to do this yourself.

God's Will for Human Relationships

Choosing a Marriage Partner

"Whom should I marry?" is one of the major decisions of life. Is this question to be approached with the assumption that you "must find the one person that God has ordained that you marry" in order to be sure that you don't make a mistake? No statement or implication in the Bible supports this common assumption. Because of this kind of thinking, I have occasionally talked to Christians whose marriage is on the rocks and heard comments like "we married outside the will of God." This is nothing but a pious cop-out that avoids the moral responsibility that comes with a decision to marry. So what does the Bible teach about God's will for making a choice for marriage?

Genesis and Jesus (Matt. 19:4–6) teach us that God's original intention was for one man and woman to be together until death. This expectation blew Jesus' disciples away (Matt. 19:10) and highlighted the solemnity of one's choice to marry. The institution of marriage and how it operates in culture surfaces throughout the Bible in both a literal and figurative way. Yet, while marriage is the normal expectation, no Bible passage calls for a mystical discovery of your "one and only." Some Old Testament texts command ethnic continuity for marriage (Deut. 7:3; Josh. 23:12–13), but these texts are only descriptive of God's will for Israel within a certain time frame. Second Corinthians 6:14–18 commands us not to "be yoked together with unbelievers." The context is not about marriage, but the principle certainly can be applied to marriage in that a believer and an unbeliever do not have the kind of common ground needed to engage in a lifetime relationship. In the case of George and Judy, the marriage was already in force and is binding. Other texts point out what constitutes a good man or woman, and the implication is that we should use such instruction as a model for our evaluation of a future mate. Proverbs 31 and Ephesians 5 reflect upon the good wife and husband. But these are texts that talk about those already married, and we often use them to reflect forward to a future mate. In fact, the Bible's focus is on evaluating and regulating existing marriages, not on making the up-front choice.

Since we have no instructional passage in the Bible on how to make this important choice, how should we proceed? We should proceed on the basis of what best maintains our worldview and values. We first seek a person with whom we have compatibility of belief and values. There will be more than one choice in this regard. Since God has not instructed us to use some mystical process to find the "only one," we are responsible to make a choice among relative equals. We can narrow the field down by evaluating personal interests and life goals, but we will still have more than one option. We can also evaluate our personal feelings, that is, whose company do we enjoy the most? In the courting stage, "love" is most likely naive infatuation. Can we identify why we are infatuated with a person? Is it because of an attraction to a physical, mental, social, or some other aspect of the person's qualities? Which of these areas reflect our core values? Can we think out to the future and ask which of the qualities of this person will we most cherish when our youthful fantasies are gone?

As important as it is, God has put the choice of whom we marry in our court. Even though he knows all the ramifications of the outcome of our choice, and even what could have been with another choice, he has not ordained a way to bypass the responsibility of making a choice. We are forced to make our choices on the basis of the biblical teaching that we have as we evaluate our own values about life. After we have made our choices and entered into the covenant of marriage, the Bible begins to teach us God's will about marriage. His will is explained in terms of the moral and social responsibilities that come with marriage and raising a family. We must find ways to continue our commitment through the changes life brings us. After a few years of marriage, the incompatibilities will begin to surface! When they do, we are not free to seek another marriage if this one develops in unexpected ways. Rather, we are responsible to cultivate the garden in which we find ourselves. Since marriage is the closest of all relationships, it will supply the most intense experiences of joy and pain. It is God's will that we grow in dealing with both.

Divorcing and Being "Single Again"

We do not live in a perfect world. The increase in the divorce rate among Christians is alarming. Yet, when we read the Old Testament, we see that Moses faced this issue over three thousand years ago.

Is it ever God's will to divorce? The answer to this question depends on one's understanding of the biblical passages that address divorce. Much ink of interpretation has been spilt over this question, and an answer that satisfies all Christians has not been achieved.[1] God's Word addresses this important question in a way that leaves believers with questions and tension over the right answer. Why does God do this to us? We must assume that he could have provided information in a way to completely avoid the discussion about "which view is right." The fact that he did not indicates that once again he uses the tension to achieve his purposes in ways that may not be as clear to us as we would desire. To delineate the views that answer the question of divorce would require another book! Therefore, for the sake of thinking about how to deal with the question, please assume with me the following answer: "All divorce is contrary to the revealed will of God." If this is true, then how do believers who have suffered this tragedy face the rest of life on earth? The answer is simple. They do what every other believer who is damaged by sin does. They apply the biblical theology of repentance, forgiveness, and restoration to their life context. Psalm 51 reflects the journey of one believer in this regard. This psalm expresses how David dealt with his sins of adultery, lying, and murder (Ps. 51: 1–12). David certainly experienced the human aftermath of the consequences of his sin, but he still found his way back into fellowship with God (vv. 10–12). He also went on to use his life experience, as bad as it was, to help others avoid the pain he had experienced (vv. 13–19).

So, how do "single again" people discern God's will about communication with their former spouse, how to deal with an estate, how to share the children, etc.? They do it on the same basis that they deal with all other decisions. They must determine how biblical teachings and values now apply to the various issues that arise in this broken relationship. While there is certainly a place for anger when the most precious of human relationships is destroyed, this characteristic cannot control one's way of dealing with the future, or life will be consumed with vengeance.

The question "What about the children?" surfaces in new ways. My wife recently hosted a number of first to third grade girls for an overnight "pajama party." I surfaced the next morning, after a good night's sleep (!), and cooked pancakes for the gang. I naively asked one of the children if she had brothers and sisters. She casually began to describe her biological family, her current stepfamily, and the new stepfamily that was coming. I felt drained as I listened and wondered how such a young mind deals with such diversity. How does God's will guide her relationships with these extended situations? How do we adults mentor children in applying God's will in a broken world? Perhaps we should read the Gospels more deeply and observe how Jesus dealt with broken and battered people.

Caring for Aging Parents

If you are fifty something, you are likely beginning to face the challenges of care for aging parents. Such decisions are often aggravated by distance and perhaps the stubbornness of a parent who will not leave the safety of familiar surroundings. My mother adamantly insisted that she was fine and needed no help, even though she could no longer pay bills, drive, shop, or cook. She was in good physical condition, but dementia was taking its toll.

The Bible tells us to "honor our parents" (Exod. 20:12). It illustrates that part of this command includes taking care of them when they cannot care for themselves. But the biblical culture and its social structures are quite different than today. Does proper care of parents mean helping them to remain in an independent setting, live in your home, or be situated in an assisted living facility? You promised them that you would never put them in a nursing home, but you never faced the complications of care before now. You and your spouse work full-time. Should one of you quit? But then how would you pay the bills? Perhaps you have children or a house that cannot accommodate everyone. Perhaps your parent is a cranky, negative person who undermines your family environment. Perhaps you and your spouse do not agree about what it means to care for the parent. Perhaps your parent is not financially stable and you must deal with the complicated healthcare system and your own family unit's stability.

It is God's will that we honor our parents. How we do so will vary depending on the answers to the above questions and many others. Every question brings different values into play. Our decisions will have to weigh the nature of these values. I once saw a family nearly destroyed because the son was blind to how his mother manipulated him against his wife and children. These are not easy decisions, but they are very real ones. Furthermore, God has not provided us with a system to bypass our own responsibility to make decisions; he has called us to engage the task of decision making.

God's Will for Career Decisions

It is God's will that we work for a living. Adam worked the Garden to provide for him and Eve prior to their sin and expulsion. We begin to prepare for a career of work from birth, especially with the start of the educational process. Therefore, making decisions about God's will for our career spans a lot of time and includes both our desires and the path our parents carve out for us.

Educating Children

Which option is God's will to educate my children? The Bible reflects the educational systems that were current with the time of its composition. The use of the Bible to promote a certain kind of educational system in modern terms likely violates the original context. Biblical writers charged parents and leaders to teach their children and followers religious truth (Deut. 11:18–21; Matt. 28:18–20; 1 Tim. 1:18; 2 Tim. 2:2), but they did not present a view of public or private education that is analogous to our modern situation. Contexts that promote religious instruction within the family and their respective worshiping communities cannot be claimed as a model for an entire educational system for all subjects of study. This was not the Bible's original intent.

Our current Christian culture utilizes three avenues to educate its children: home school models, private institutions (including parochial schools), and the public education system (including charter schools). To decide which of these is God's will for you and your children will require that you once again apply your worldview and values system to the options. Because education is so value-laden, this issue will bring a lot of conflicting opinions to the table. Issues will range from the quality of education to the need for the socialization experience of the child. For example, in some geographical regions, the public school system is liberal and anti-Christian. In other parts of the country, however, it may be largely staffed by Christians and therefore user-friendly for the church community. Home school may seem to be a way to protect your children from liberal and sinful social influences, but if you, as the teacher, are not prepared educationally for the broad range of subjects for which you are responsible, will you rob your children of their future ability to compete in a job market? Is there value in putting children into an environment unfriendly to Christian truth (e.g., public education) so that they can learn to cope with the real world while you are still present to guide them? How do we weigh the commands to influence our world for the gospel? Sometimes Christian schools seem safer, but they contain some young people from Christian homes who are sick of restrictions and more aggressive about breaking the rules than some of their secular counterparts. If you have the availability of these three options, each will have its strengths and weaknesses for your situation, and your final decision must weigh which is best overall. You may also find your options change with geography and grade level. Therefore, you must be vigilant in your decision-making process.

Choosing a Place for Higher Education

Next to marriage, our decision about preparation for a lifetime of work may be our most important choice. I have often heard young people graduating from high school speak about seeking God's guidance about the choice of a major field for their college education. So how should a young person go about choosing a school or field of study? Our sample chart on decision making noted a number of issues important for this process (see figure 7 on page 65). Critical self-awareness is crucial. Students should pursue their dreams, but when they flunk chemistry repeatedly, it is a good sign that being physicians is not God's will for them. Many young people change majors as they gain a deeper understanding of who they are. The counsel of informed people and friends is important, but listening is often not a skill of youth. One's personal maturity will influence this category a great deal. The item most often applied to the decision is personal desires. What motivates and captures the attention of a young person changes quickly. But with time and experience, a theme begins to emerge. We should allow our young people to go through this roller-coaster process. We should also be supportive as a theme begins to emerge to help them see how their life's interest is surfacing. Within this context, God's will for their life's work is best pursued. Prayer and godly living is the umbrella that keeps people focused throughout this process, but in the unfolding process, young people discern the answer to the questions about their life's work.

In spite of how careful we may have been in our early decision making, sometimes our reflection in hindsight brings a level of pain. I am an educator by profession. I am well aware of the strengths and weaknesses of higher education. When I reflect on my own journey, I realize that if I had the advantage of hindsight, I would make some decisions differently. I realize that sometimes I did not listen well to a few people who gave me good advice. Now I give advice to younger persons who also have flawed hearing! Yet we cannot redo the past. My own worldview reminds me that even though my decisions were conditioned by the limitations of where I was in my life's journey at a given point, those decisions were within God's moral will and divine providence. I am the person that I am because of that journey. God has and is accomplishing his purposes in my life within that journey. As the saying goes, "Good judgment comes from experience and a lot of experience comes from poor judgment." If we are able honestly to evaluate our journey, we will discover that our poor judgment often taught us the most. God's plan includes this learning aspect.

God's Will for Church Relationships

Choosing a Church

The choice of a church is a major decision. The New Testament presents believers gathering together in local groups for worship, for observance of the ordinances, and for fellowship. From this pattern, we derive the truth that we should attach ourselves to a specific group of believers.

This is God's will; however, the great variety of available churches complicates our choice. Issues of theology and governance need careful consideration, although I have observed that these areas are not on the minds of Christians as much as they used to be. How the pulpit and Sunday school system mentors you in biblical teaching are crucial to your spiritual growth. How a church is or is not governed can be a cause of much frustration. Your status in life, whether single, married, or married with children, and how each church addresses these needs will play heavily into your evaluation. The abilities that God has blessed you with for work in the church should be considered as you evaluate the needs of the churches that you investigate. You should also compare your personal values, such as relational warmth and honesty, to the churches you are considering.

I have met many believers who can never settle on a church home. Some are looking for the "perfect" church in all categories. I don't think it ever dawns on some folks that if they joined the "perfect" church, it would then cease to be perfect! A speaker I once heard made a wise statement about choosing a church. "Don't look for a church with no problems, look for one that has problems with which you can deal!" Make a decision and work with it.

Making a Church Change

We live in a culture that is driven by the word *change*. Adults often change jobs freely and make more major career shifts than at any time in the past. We are a mobile society, and that breeds change. In fact, change has become a value in some business communities. The regular rotation of managers is supposed to spark creativity and productivity. The winds of change have affected both the leaders and members of the church. The Barna Research Group has specialized in tracking church and ministerial trends since 1984. Barna's data, as early as 1990, reflects that "change" affects both lay and vocational ministers.[2] Barna's June 2002 data lists the median length of a senior pastor's ministry in a given church as four years. If ministers change so quickly, what influence does that have on the attitudes of parishioners?

So when we feel the urge to make a change in the church we attend, how do we discern God's will? I often hear believers use the feeling of "a need for change" as divine guidance. Rather, we should first be conscious of the fact that we live in a world that uses change to achieve personal happiness. No more than a fish feels wet do we feel the subtle influences of our culture. Our only defense against being like our world is to know its characteristics. No direct biblical texts address the question of changing churches. Although 1 Corinthians and John's third Epistle reflect how rival groups existed at an early stage and they each probably had their own "congregations," the Bible does not reflect these groups in a positive light. The scenery has changed over the centuries. We now have numerous choices of churches that are quite different in theology and practice, although they are within the camp of orthodox belief. It serves no useful purpose to argue whether the variety of denominations is valid. The fact is that they exist and we must make a choice. So we are back to the issue of applying our biblical understanding and the values we derive from that understanding to the decisions we face. One value to consider when confronted with making a church change is "loyalty." The idea of loyalty has diminished in our culture. The mobility of our culture and an overemphasis on individual happiness often leads us to ignore being loyal in spite of difficulties. On the other hand, loyalty can also be used to manipulate adherents. I personally value loyalty until there are compelling reasons to make a move. These reasons do occur, and each of us must decide when they do and take responsibility before God for our actions. Most "compelling reasons" will fall in the areas of personal convictions and values. My experience is that theology is usually not why people make a change, although that would certainly be a reason. Personality conflicts, church governance, music programs, poor preaching, and poor youth ministries are common reasons. Perhaps you have made a change so that you can avoid conflict in one of these or other areas. As long as frank and loving conversations about issues have occurred, a change could be appropriate. It does not serve biblical values, however, to make a change in order to avoid such conversations.

God's Will for Life Stewardship

Believers in the God of the Bible in every age live in light of the truth that belief in God is a lifestyle. Gathering with other believers at set times during the week does not completely fulfill our stewardship to God. Add to those meetings the performance of all of the spiritual disciplines and you still come up short. We are believers 24/7. Being a Christian is a philosophy of life, not just one of our activities. In fact, some perform all of the activities but are empty inside. Bible-believing people must address how all of their time and resources are a stewardship to God.

The Stewardship of Time

Garth had a stable vocation as an automobile worker, but playing the acoustic guitar and singing was his avocation. After becoming a Christian, he struggled with whether it was God's will for him to continue to devote time to the music he loved. His music was within the boundaries of God's moral will, but should he spend time doing this when there were so many needs within his local church. Because he loved playing and singing so much, he sometimes struggled with a sense of guilt over the time he invested in this activity.

How would you counsel Garth? Would you tell him that "leisure time" is not an option for the Christian? Would you suggest to him, "We work to survive and be responsible citizens, but after that we are bound to do church/religious activities only"? Or would you say, "Hey man, do whatever turns you on!" I think both of these approaches miss the point. Living the Christian life does not mean compartmentalizing our activities. Statements like "Whatever you do, do it all for the glory of God" (1 Cor. 10:31), and "God . . . richly provides us with everything for our enjoyment" (1 Tim. 6:17), teach us that each part of our lives is a gift from God and we may freely exercise any area as long as we do it within divine boundaries. King David paid a lot of dues to music practice before he was recognized as the sweet singer of Israel. The apostle Paul spent adequate time watching athletic events to be conversant enough to freely use this domain as an illustration about Christian living. It is not God's will for us to divide our lives into secular and sacred categories. Rather, we are called to integrate all of life with our stewardship to God.

There are many Garths in the world. For some it is music, for others, sports, and the list goes on and on. We do not find God's permission or justification for our activities by seeking a subjective confirmation or denial. Instead, we exercise all of our gifts and desires in a manner that is balanced and glorifying to God.

The Stewardship of Money

I am writing this book in the midst of the disclosures of how deeply the leaders of American companies lied and "cooked the books" to make their company's financial bottom lines look better than they were. While I do not know any persons connected with Enron, Adelphia, or World.com, I am sure there are some Christian employees. The shareholders and employees of these companies lost millions of dollars in investments during 2002. Hundreds, perhaps thousands, of lives were devastated. How should the believers who were hurt by these companies view their decisions to invest their monies there? Should they blame God for not warning them? Or would God avoid divulging such information since that would break the "insider trading" law! I think most Christians would do a lot of introspection and wonder if they failed spiritually to discern God's will. I consider all of these answers to be inadequate. The persons who have been hurt by the sins of their leaders did what all responsible people do. They planned for the future. They acted like responsible future retirees and stewards of the resources God entrusted to them. I would assume that the believers in the group reflected and prayed about how to be good stewards. They followed what appeared at the time to be the appropriate course of action. But they were betrayed by the greed and sinful self-protection of their leaders. They now suffer, not because of their actions, but because of the sins of others. This is the kind of world we live in, and God usually does not intervene to deliver us from it. We have to apply God's moral will even in the aftermath of tragedy. Read how the psalmists and writers of the Proverbs struggled with the pain of living in a sinful world. They prayed that God would bring justice upon wrongdoers while he gave the victims the grace to endure. Their prayers were often presented in the midst of suffering for doing the will of God.

God's Will for Special Issues

I have placed a number of questions into categories for the sake of organizational convenience. As believers, we face many additional issues in our fallen world. Questions related to civil government, life and death issues in an advanced medical system, the unique nature of the American legal system in contrast to the biblical world, and many other issues face us daily. As our culture advances, our choices become more complex. The difference in issues now from the biblical world of two thousand years ago highlights the need to study Scripture in order to develop a biblical worldview and values mindset. A simple proof-text approach will not provide us with the answers we seek. God never intended that the Bible be a comprehensive proof-text reference manual for every imaginable occasion that would arise. It did not even do this for the redeemed community during its composition! Rather, the Bible is a story of God's dealings with the redeemed community in their time and space. He has forced us into the laboratory of his Word to derive how we should think about our world today and its changing issues. The Bible is fully sufficient for everything we need to know if we will pursue its lead. The church as a community must diligently evaluate the issues of life and apply a biblical worldview and values set to the questions it faces. While we make decisions as individuals, certain seminal issues must be more than an individual believer's task, or we fall back into the privatized mindset of Western culture. The church as a community must rise as a voice to address many of the unique issues I have cited above.

As I bring this chapter to a close, I would like to reflect upon the issue of the church and its discernment of pastoral leadership.

The Call to Ministry

What is a "call to ministry" and how does a church choose a pastor? How does a believer answer the question "Is it God's will for me to pursue vocational Christian ministry?" How do we in a church deal with people who present themselves and claim, "I am called to be a pastor, please ordain me to ministry."

The New Testament is quite clear about what constitutes a "call to ministry." First Timothy 3 addresses this issue. Two elements are present: first, the applicant's burning desire to do vocational ministry, and second, the church's judgment that he is qualified. The context is also clear: it is the church that decides whether one is called, not just the desire of the one who claims a call. The experience of the call is not a vision or mystical experience. It is first the conscious nagging inner drive that will not permit one to do anything else. Then it is the development of that person within a believing community that demonstrates the correlation of claimed call and giftedness. So in this case, God's will is determined by the consensus of the community.

The nondenominational and independent church movement in America has particularly faced the challenge of persons who claim to be called to ministry and sometimes apply this claim in spite of advice from their home church. This same movement also faces unique challenges in appointing a new pastor when they go through pastoral changes. While denominations have an established process to credential candidates for ministry and a system to help churches in their pastoral searches, many independent groups struggle with pastoral changes.

Choosing a partner for marriage is a good analogy to illustrate calling a pastor. Just as the New Testament delineates the qualities of husbands and wives, so the qualities and gifts of a pastor are delineated in the Epistles. A church should review these texts to understand what to seek in its leader. As the personality compatibility of a man and woman is crucial for a marriage, so it is for a pastor and a congregation. Opposites may be infatuated with each other for a while, but over time the differences become aggravating. The compatibility of goals and how to achieve them are important for a good match in both marriage and the calling of a pastor. In other words, a church needs to think deeply and clearly about its identity and what it wants to be in order to search for a person who is following the same direction. The church matches its values with the values of candidates. Trauma results when a good match is not achieved. Neither is the work of the church advanced. A pastor should not be chosen merely on a brief pulpit experience and a superficial question-and-answer session. No amount of prayer or "feelings" will avert the disaster of a thoughtless choice.

Conclusion

In considering these life questions, I have endeavored to think out loud in a manner suggestive of the process you should go through when confronted with life's issues. I would challenge you to take these questions and begin to develop *your* answers. I have purposefully only been suggestive because, at the end of the day, one cannot deal with life by seeking a quick fix from someone else. If an answer to a question about God's will is not your own, when your answer is challenged, you will not be able to stand your ground. Your confidence about how to deal with life's issues will be unstable.

God expects each of his children to take the responsibility to develop and apply a biblical worldview and values set. This is not an easy task. There are no shortcuts. But when you invest yourself in this kind of growth, and experience the confidence of settled convictions about your decisions, the reward is far greater than the labor.

Conclusion

One of the most common remarks that I receive when I teach about knowing God's will is: "I finally feel free to make decisions!" Many have approached knowing God's will as some sort of mystical process to procure divine guidance before making a decision. This approach leaves people in a state of limbo. They are looking for some undefined inner impression in order to make a decision. This impression is supposed to give them confidence to move in a certain direction. When people come to understand that knowing God's will is a matter of obeying God's moral will and applying a biblical worldview and values set to all other decisions, they feel free to make a decision—they have an objective framework in which to process their questions. They are free from the fear of making a mistake or "missing God's will," because as long as they operate within the parameters of God's moral will they know that God is present and doing a work in their lives. Furthermore, throughout history, "God often builds our character and his work on our mistakes."

Another comment is: "I didn't realize how crucial it is to know the Bible. My Bible has become a much larger and influential book." When Christians cannot locate a proof text to address a question, they often assume the Bible does not address that need. We have observed that the Bible is a story of God's dealings with the redeemed community over the ages. It is not a manual that directly addresses every imaginable question that might arise. The Bible's total sufficiency for the faith and practice of a believer rests in taking its teaching to the next level. God's Word not only teaches specifically in its various contexts but also provides leadership in developing a biblical worldview and values set. We consider what it implies and how we can organize its teaching to address the larger questions we have. The Bible of many Christians is virtually unused. Some tend to run their lives on impressions that come to them rather than by a reasoned system of decision making. If you have understood the model presented in this book, you should feel overwhelmed with your responsibility to gain a greater understanding of the Scripture and how to extend the application of its teaching to the issues of life.

Persons who have exercised a mystical approach "to find God's will" sometimes feel that there is not enough God, prayer, or the Spirit in this model. Given the subjective presuppositions that drive such models, I can understand that they do not find what they seek in a values-driven model. But I firmly believe that the values-driven model drives us to God in a way that he designed. First, our access to God in the realm of knowledge is his Word. I'm sure you have seen how I value the Bible. I cannot separate valuing the Bible from valuing God's mind. This is how God ordained to communicate to every generation. It is our only objective source of knowledge about God and his will. When a model about knowing God's will emphasizes subjective communication from God over careful study of Scripture, it has undermined the very way God has chosen to communicate to us! When we pray, "Sir, we would see Jesus," then we need to see him by reading the Gospels, for therein he is fully revealed.

Secondly, my model drives me to pray. My prayer focuses on a plea for help and protection in ways I will never know as I fulfill my responsibility for the life God has given me to live. I pray earnestly for the Spirit's conviction and my sensitivity to that conviction as I process decisions. I believe a model of discernment that depends on worldview and values development requires an intense experience in all of these domains.

If you feel disappointed that I have not adequately addressed enough questions, good! My purpose is to point you in a direction that will enable you to seek and find your answers. You may feel inadequate for this task. You may feel lost in a book as large as the Bible. Don't give up; begin the journey! This is God's will for you.

Notes

Chapter 1

1. Harold H. Titus, Marilyn S. Smith, and Richard T. Nolan, *Living Issues in Philosophy*, 7th ed. (New York: D. Van Nostrand Company, 1979), 174.

2. Walter C. Kaiser Jr., "A Neglected Text in Bibliology Discussions: 1 Corinthians 2:6–16," *Westminster Theological Journal* 43 (1981): 301–19.

3. The theme that our decisions require critical reflection from a Christian worldview base is also well stated in a recently published book that arrived on my desk too late to be incorporated into my writing. Please see Dennis P. Hollinger, *Choosing the Good: Christian Ethics in a Complex World* (Grand Rapids: Baker, 2002), especially part 3.

Chapter 2

1. *The Westminster Confession of Faith*, VI.6.

2. Ronald H. Nash, *Faith and Reason: Searching for a Rational Faith* (Grand Rapids: Zondervan, 1988), see part 1 on "The Christian World-View."

3. Cf. Brian J. Walsh and J. Richard Middleton, *The Transforming Vision: Shaping a Christian World View* (Downers Grove, Ill.: InterVarsity Press, 1984), 33.

Chapter 3

1. Weston Fields, "The Sodom Tradition in Intertestamental and New Testament Literature," in Gary T. Meadors, ed., *New Testament Essays in Honor of Homer A. Kent, Jr.* (Winona Lake, Ind.: BMH Books, 1991), 35–48.

2. Frederick William Danker, ed., *A Greek-English Lexicon of the New Testament and Other Early Christian Literature* [BDAG], 3rd ed. (Chicago: University of Chicago Press, 2000), 525a.

3. Ibid., 168a.

Chapter 4

1. Chou Wee Pan, "Fool [entry 211]" in Willem Van Gemeren, ed., *New International Dictionary of Old Testament Theology and Exegesis*, vol. 1 (Grand Rapids: Zondervan, 1997), 306–9.

2. For more information about divination in the Ancient Near East, see I. Mendelsohn, "Divination" in George A. Buttrick, ed., *The Interpreter's Dictionary of the Bible*, vol. 1 (Nashville: Abingdon Press,1962), 586–88; Bruce Waltke, *Finding the Will of God: A Pagan Notion?* (Gresham, Oreg.: Vision House, 1995), 41–58; and Frederick H. Cryer, *Divination in Ancient Israel and Its Near Eastern Environment* (Sheffield, England: Sheffield Academic Press, 1994).

3. Cornelis Van Dam, *The Urim and Thummim: A Means of Revelation in Ancient Israel* (Winona Lake, Ind.: Eisenbrauns, 1997), 254.

Chapter 5

1. See F. H. Klooster, "Sovereignty of God" in Walter A. Elwell, ed., *Evangelical Dictionary of Theology* (Grand Rapids: Baker, 1984),1038–39.

Chapter 6

1. See Walter C. Kaiser Jr., *Toward Old Testament Ethics* (Grand Rapids: Zondervan, 1983).

2. See the discussion of Leviticus 11 in Gordon J. Wenham, *The Book of Leviticus* (Grand Rapids: Eerdmans, 1979).

Chapter 7

1. See Michael Wittmer, *Heaven Is a Place on Earth* (forthcoming. Grand Rapids: Zondervan, 2004); Albert M. Wolters, *Creation Regained: Biblical Basis for a Reformational Worldview* (Grand Rapids: Eerdmans, 1985); and James W. Sire, *The Universe Next Door: A Basic Worldview Catalog* (Downers Grove, Ill.: InterVarsity Press, 1997).

Chapter 8

1. I memorized the phrasing "the norms and values that we recognize and apply" from F. F. Bruce many years ago but cannot cite the source.

2. For another description, see Gary T. Meadors, "Conscience," in Walter A. Elwell, ed., *The Evangelical Dictionary of Biblical Theology* (Grand Rapids: Baker Books, 1996).

Chapter 9

1. Raymond E. Brown, *The Epistles of John*. The Anchor Bible, vol. 30 (New York: Doubleday, 1982), 341–50

2. See B. B. Warfield, "The Leading of the Spirit," in *Biblical and Theological Studies* (Philadelphia: Presbyterian and Reformed Publishing Company, 1952); and John Murray, "The Guidance of the Holy Spirit," in *Collected Writings of John Murray*, vol. 1 (Edinburgh: Banner of Truth Trust, 1976).

3. I hold that the "miraculous gifts" that were the property of individuals, which were not a direct act of God alone, ceased with the apostolic age. For common views about these kinds of gifts, see Wayne A. Grudem, ed., *Are Miraculous Gifts for Today? Four Views* (Grand Rapids: Zondervan, 1996).

Chapter 10

1. Terrance Tiessen, *Providence and Prayer: How Does God Work in the World?* (Downers Grove, Ill.: InterVarsity Press, 2000).

Chapter 11

1. You will have to read a variety of books to begin to form your view of divorce. I would suggest that you start with William A. Heth and Gordon J. Wenham, *Jesus and Divorce: The Problem with the Evangelical Consensus* (Nashville: Thomas Nelson, 1985). This volume will give you an overview of most of the options for interpreting divorce passages.

2. George Barna, *The Church Today: Insightful Statistics and Commentary* (Glendale, Calif.: Barna Research Group, 1990). See the Barna web site for further information: www.barna.org.

Selected Bibliography

Buttrick, George A., ed. *The Interpreter's Dictionary of the Bible*. 5 volumes. Nashville: Abingdon Press, 1962.

Elwell, Walter A., ed. *Evangelical Dictionary of Theology*. Grand Rapids: Baker, 1984.

Friesen, Garry. *Decision Making and the Will of God: A Biblical Alternative to the Traditional View*. Portland: Multnomah, 1980.

Hollinger, Dennis P. *Choosing the Good: Christian Ethics in a Complex World*. Grand Rapids: Baker, 2002.

Kaiser, Walter C. "A Neglected Text in Bibliology Discussions: 1 Corinthians 2:6–16." *Westminster Theological Journal* 43 (1981): 301–19.

———. *Toward Old Testament Ethics*. Grand Rapids: Zondervan, 1983.

Milco, Michael R. *Ethical Dilemmas in Church Leadership: Case Studies in Biblical Decision Making*. Grand Rapids: Kregel, 1997.

Nash, Ronald H. *Faith and Reason: Searching for a Rational Faith*. Grand Rapids: Zondervan, 1988.

Sire, James W. *The Universe Next Door: A Basic Worldview Catalog*. Downers Grove, Ill.: InterVarsity Press, 1997.

Smith, M. Blaine. *Knowing God's Will: Biblical Principles of Guidance.* Downers Grove, Ill.: InterVarsity Press, 1979.

Titus, Harold H., Marilyn S. Smith, and Richard T. Nolan. *Living Issues in Philosophy.* 7th ed. New York: D. Van Nostrand Company, 1979.

Van Dam, Cornelis. *The Urim and Thummim: A Means of Revelation in Ancient Israel.* Winona Lake, Ind.: Eisenbrauns, 1997.

Van Gemeren, Willem, ed. *New International Dictionary of Old Testament Theology and Exegesis.* 5 volumes. Grand Rapids: Zondervan, 1997.

Walsh, Brian J. and J. Richard Middleton. *The Transforming Vision: Shaping a Christian World View.* Downers Grove, Ill.: InterVarsity Press, 1984.

Waltke, Bruce. *Finding the Will of God: A Pagan Notion?* Gresham, Oreg.: Vision House, 1995.

Wolters, Albert M. *Creation Regained: Biblical Basis for a Reformational Worldview.* Grand Rapids: Eerdmans, 1985.

Gary T. Meadors, Th.D., is professor of Greek and New Testament at Grand Rapids Theological Seminary of Cornerstone University in Michigan.